THE PLAIN TRUTH ABOUT ARMSTRONG-ISM

THE PLAIN TRUTH ABOUT ARMSTRONG- ISM

Roger R. Chambers

D. Edmond Hiebert
Collection

BAKER BOOK HOUSE
Grand Rapids, Michigan

Library of Congress Catalog Card Number:

ISBN: 0-8010-2337-8

PRINTED IN THE UNITED STATES OF AMERICA

PREFACE

The spiritual vacuum of the twentieth century is the inevitable womb of a durable cultism, and few cults are flourishing more than Armstrongism. *The Plain Truth* and lately *Tomorrow's World* magazines have become household items for thousands of Americans. As of 1969 Ambassador College Press claimed a monthly circulation of more than 1,610,000 for *The Plain Truth*. The radio voice of Armstrongism, "The World Tomorrow," is heard on more than three hundred stations. The multilingual publications and broadcasts reach Canada, Europe, Asia, the Caribbean and Latin American countries, and other areas by shortwave. The television log is growing rapidly. The Worldwide Church of God (formerly the Radio Church of God) meets in cities throughout the world every Saturday.

It thus may seem a contradiction to affirm that the doctrines of Armstrongism are relatively unknown, but such is the case. The Worldwide Church of God regularly meets in unlabeled rented halls behind locked doors. The services are led by ministers who are not listed in city directories as clergymen, and who often have unlisted phone numbers. The public is not encouraged to attend. Many activities of the cult are carried on incognito, the desire being to appear as a patriotic or some other kind of nonreligious group. Many a church leader has had the rude awakening of finding that some of the faithful have been lost to a religious system so bizarre that he is totally unprepared to answer the audacious claims with which he is faced. He quickly finds that indignant bluster does not serve as an adequate response to the specious arguments of Armstrongism.

Armstrongism is presented to the public in a very convincing way. Madison Avenue has never offered a more efficient hard-sell. The publications rolling off the Ambassador College presses are of first quality. The magazines contain excellent material on evolution, drug-abuse, pollution, morals, and so forth. There is much in what is voiced abroad by "The World Tomorrow" that is to be appreciated by the person who loves God and truth.

But the broadcasts are seldom given to explaining the specific teachings of the sect. The format is skillfully designed to capture the attention of the general public. Never is a hymn played. Never is a prayer made. Scintillating questions are asked. Few clear answers are given. Two principal objectives are achieved by the extensive radio and television ministry. They are (a) the enhancement of the reputation of Armstrongism by the presentation of material universally admitted to be wholesome, and (b) the prompting of the public to write to the Pasadena address. Thousands are writing. Thousands are being contacted by Armstrongite ministers and are becoming affiliated with the Worldwide Church of God. Other thousands who would never seriously consider leaving their present church enthusiastically read the printed matter and regularly send money.

It will never do to simply hack at the branches of Armstrongism. It is a waste of time to heap scorn upon isolated theological aberrations. Label the lost tribes hunting expedition through the British Isles religious myth and fantasy, and you will quickly find that men want that kind of thing to be true. For years the Mormon Church has prospered in the polytheistic "God Family" doctrine of God, the Holy Spirit, and salvation. Men have always wanted to be God. The first temptation that came to mankind was an invitation to be a part of the "God Family" (Gen. 3:5). It is not a vulnerable point in Armstrongism. The Jehovah's Witnesses have long since proved that men want to be persuaded that there is no hell. This is not the place to begin on Armstrongism. It is astonishing that the ancient Ebionite error concerning the Law and the Sabbath can enjoy both resurrection and survival through Seventh-Day Adventism in the same world that has access to the New Testament. If the Adventist error can survive the Epistle to the Galatians, the Armstrongite version of it will be as durable. Armstrong's doctrine of the throne of David is dispensationalism. One dispensationalist can never refute another. Those expecting a literal throne in Jerusalem over a temporal kingdom at the Second Coming must "Amen" Armstrong up to the point of the identification of "Israel." This explains the overwhelming ineffectiveness of interdenominational dispensationalism in dealing with Armstrongism. The prevalence of dispensationalism in general indicates the tenacity of the ancient Jewish error of the misapplication of Old Testament prophecy. It has survived the clear teachings of Jesus and the apostles. It is not an obvious breach in the wall of Armstrongite error.

The roots of the Armstrongite heresy go deep. The taproot is exposed in the book *The United States and British Commonwealth in Prophecy*. The book does not elaborate all the doctrines of the cult. But if the material in it cannot withstand a critical examination, Armstrongism is destroyed. In no uncertain terms Armstrong claims that the identification of the United States and Great Britain in prophecy is the long-lost "key" to the understanding of the Bible. This identification is logically and admittedly the key to Armstrongism.

The primary purpose of this book is to examine the key and see if it fits the lock. Basic Armstrongism is scrutinized. It must be recognized that a work which effectively handled every part of the Armstrongite theological structure would be encyclopedic. The availability of Scripture makes such a work unnecessary.

Sincere appreciation is expressed to those who have given aid and encouragement in the preparation of the manuscript. The author worked under the direction of Dr. James Smith of the Cincinnati Bible Seminary. Dr. Smith gave generously of his time, and the benefit of his keen scholarship to the work has been of inestimable value. Gratitude is expressed to one of God's noblemen, James M. Phillips, who gave the author valuable material that had been collected in a study of British-Israelism. Mr. Phillips is an evangelist in British Columbia. Mr. and Mrs. Corbin Cornett, Jr. of Hamilton, Ohio worked very hard in checking the manuscript for grammar and punctuation and in the typing of the final draft.

It is the prayer of us all that this book will be a help to those honestly seeking the truth.

ROGER R. CHAMBERS

Hamilton, Ohio

A RÉSUMÉ OF ARMSTRONGISM

If this book is of interest to you, it is because you have heard "The World Tomorrow" broadcast or you have been reading *The Plain Truth*. If this is the extent of your association with the organization of Herbert W. Armstrong, then you do not have a complete picture of Armstrongism. Many of the tenets of Armstrongism are not explained until after a person is already sold on the system. Following is a brief summary of the doctrines and policies of the Worldwide Church of God:

1. The message of Armstrongism began with Mrs. Herbert W. Armstrong. An angel revealed God's way to her and she shared the revelation with her husband.

2. Herbert W. Armstrong is a prophet. He disavows the distinction, but the concept of the prophet describes precisely his position in the theology of the Worldwide Church of God. The "I never claimed to be a prophet" theme is being heard more of late. This is probably prompted by the miserable failure of the main body of bold and incontrovertible predictions made "by God's direction and authority" during the last two decades. (This will in no way diminish the force of Armstrongism. Cults thrive on prophecy gone awry.) When the claims of Herbert W. Armstrong are sorted out and listed, and when the veneration paid him by his constituency is analyzed, it adds up to Prophet. What Joseph Smith is to Mormonism, Armstrong is to the Worldwide Church of God. His ministry is a fulfillment of prophecy. Ninety

percent of all Bible prophecies hinge upon the beginning of his radio and literature ministry.

3. Any objection to Armstrongite doctrine is officially labeled "persecution." All non-Armstrong churches are satanic.

4. There is not one God, but two: God the Father, the *Possessor* of heaven and earth, the Father of Jesus Christ; and the God of Abraham, Isaac, and Jacob, the active *Creator* of heaven and earth—the One who became Jesus Christ.

5. The Holy Spirit is an impersonal force.

6. Through character growth in obedience to the government of God one can be saved at the return of Jesus; that is, he can become a part of the God Family and be on equal terms with the two current members. In the "Wonderful World Tomorrow" immortals (God) will reign over a world of mortals. Abraham, Moses, and Elijah will rule over the world with Jesus; David and the apostles over Israel; Daniel and Paul over the Gentile nations. Joseph will be responsible for economy, agriculture, industry, commerce, and technology. Job will be in charge of urban renewal. He is well-fitted for this task since he built the Great Pyramid (standard pyramidology).

7. The resurrected body of Jesus was not the same one that was nailed to the cross.

8. The blood of Christ does not save a man. It simply erases past sins. Present and future salvation is a matter of keeping the Law.

9. Man has no immortal soul or spirit. He goes to neither heaven nor hell. There is no hell but the grave. Men will have a second chance after death to repent. No one knows what happens to the Christian at death.

10. Anglo-Saxons are lost Israel. The throne of England is the throne of David. All non-Saxons are inferior. Strict segregation is the plan of God. Racial intermarriage is sin. When Christ returns, Noah will be given the task of resegregating the races.

11. The Law of Moses is, for the most part, still to be observed. Passover, the days of unleavened bread, Pentecost, and the holy days are ordained by God forever and are to be kept. No farming permitted every seventh year. Christians should not wear clothing of mixed fabric.

12. Easter, Christmas, birthdays, and so forth, are not to be observed, as they are of pagan origin.

13. Armstrong requires three tithes of members. One to Pasadena. One for feasts and holy days. Every third year a third tithe is required. The claim that he never solicits money applies only to non-members. But these people are repeatedly made aware of financial needs if they are on the mailing list. The spirit of sacrifice thus required is not shared by the Armstrongs, as they enjoy lush surroundings in Pasadena, including a splendid mansion and a private jet.

14. Selective morality is the order of the day. Drugs, smoking, and lust are forbidden. Alcoholic beverages and dancing are acceptable.

15. This is Satan's world, not God's world. Therefore Christians are not responsible for keeping any more of the laws of society than necessary to stay out of the courts. The Christian is in no way to attempt to improve Satan's world. He cannot vote. He cannot serve in the armed forces. He must not belong to the P.T.A. and promote a pagan system of education. (School buildings are nevertheless regularly used for meetings and occasions that include consumption of alcoholic beverages.)

16. Physicians and medicines are forbidden. Only wine, anointing oil, and natural juices are permitted. Injections are not allowed, even for rabies.

17. If a person becomes a part of the Worldwide Church of God and his mate does not, he must be prepared to separate from the mate.

18. Followers are forbidden to answer questions about their religion unless the question comes from a person desiring to join the Worldwide Church of God.

Inquiries from all others must be referred to an expert.

19. The prophecy of the destruction of Jerusalem in Luke 21:22-24 refers only "typically" to the Jewish captivity of 70 A.D. It refers "primarily" to our future. The Roman Empire is to reappear about 1973 and the world will enter into the "tribulation." Armstrongites must be prepared to follow Mr. Armstrong to Petra in Transjordan where God's Church will be sheltered until the return of Jesus.

CONTENTS

1 THE LOST KEY

Herbert W. Armstrong claims no less prophetic authority than that of Moses or John the Baptist. Jesus asked the question of His enemies, "The baptism of John, whence was it? from heaven, or of men?" (Matt. 21:25). Armstrong, in no uncertain terms, affirms that his ministry is from heaven. He explains:

> For two 19-year time cycles the original apostles did proclaim this Gospel, the Gospel of the Kingdom of God, but in A.D. 69 they fled. In A.D. 70 came the military siege against Jerusalem. The ministers of Satan had wormed their way in, had gained such power that by persecution of political influence they were able to brand the true people of God as heretics and prevent further organized proclaiming of the same Gospel Christ brought from God. For eighteen and one-half centuries that gospel was not preached. The world was deceived into accepting a false gospel. Today Christ has raised up His work and once again allotted two 19-year time cycles for proclaiming His same Gospel, preparatory to His Second Coming. . . . *The World Tomorrow* and *The Plain Truth* are Christ's instruments which He is powerfully using. Yes, His message is shocking today. Once again it is the voice in the wilderness of religious confusion![1]

[1] *The Inside Story of the World Tomorrow Broadcast,* pp. 7-11.

He insists that "by God's direction and authority, I have laid the TRUTH before you!"[2]

In approaching Armstrongism, it is critical and pivotal that one understand his position as to the singular prophetic significance of his message. He acknowledges no debt to any previous religious system. He emphatically denies that his doctrine is an outgrowth of established theologies. Follow his argument:

1. The true gospel has not been preached for eighteen and one-half centuries.

2. God has raised up the ministry of the Radio Church of God to preach the message that has not been preached since the death of the apostles, that of the coming kingdom.

3. The "key" that opens the Bible to human understanding had been lost, but has been discovered by himself.

4. It is logical and necessary for the key to have been unavailable, for "the prophecies of Daniel were sealed and closed up until now"[3] ("latter half of the Twentieth Century").[4]

5. God revealed the key to Armstrong; hence he and he alone can reveal the truth of revelation, all the rest of the world being in "total ignorance."[5] The work of the Worldwide Church of God is the only one recognized by God today.

Thus the logical and inevitable conclusion of Armstrong's implied syllogism is that his system stands or falls on whether or not it is true that the master key had been lost. If Armstrongism has the market cornered on truth because he has had access to the key to the Bible,

2 Herbert W. Armstrong, *The United States and British Commonwealth In Prophecy* (Pasadena, Calif.: Ambassador Press, 1967), p. 212.

3 *Ibid.*, p. 6.

4 *Ibid.*

5 *Ibid.*

then it follows that if someone else had or has the key, they too would be "in" on the mysteries of revelation. If it can be demonstrated that the key has not only been available, but has been repeatedly and desperately twisted in the lock, then Armstrong is proved a false prophet. This is why Armstrong denies any debt to previous religious systems. The key cannot be both a second-hand theory and a revelation from heaven. If the prophecies of Daniel were sealed until the latter half of the twentieth century, then the key to their understanding could not have been lying around, available for general use, before that time.

When Jesus asked the question about the baptism of John, His enemies would have been off the hook if John had been practicing a traditional form of Jewish ceremonial cleansing. Everyone would have known it if that had been the case. If they had said, "Oh, John is just an Essene and they all baptize like that," the multitude would have known they were lying; and they feared the multitude because they believed that John was a prophet. They would not have believed that if John had been preaching and practicing a second-hand religious rite. And so if Armstrong is going to preserve the fantasy that his version of "The Plain Truth" is by "God's direction and authority," he can never admit that the key was revealed to him from any source but heaven. The proposition of the lost key is the *sine qua non* of Armstrongism, and he knows it. If this cornerstone of his theology does not hold up, then Armstrongism crumbles.

At the risk of being repetitious, let us again emphasize the fact that the pivotal issue is not the question of the accuracy of his system of Biblical interpretation, but the question of its absolute uniqueness. There is no *logical* necessity of proving that the key does not fit the lock in order to brand Armstrong a deceiver. There is only the necessity of proving that the key has not been lost since the time of the apostles. Hypothetically and logically, a man could stand up and preach a message in

17

perfect harmony with Scripture, and be an obvious fraud by virtue of the claim that he did not read it in Scripture but was given the message in a direct supernatural revelation.

British-Israelism

The substructure and foundation of Armstrongism is British-Israelism (also called Anglo-Israelism). The identification of the Anglo-Saxon peoples as "lost Israel" is the fabled key to the Bible. Armstrong denies any connection with or indebtedness to traditional and historic British-Israelism. The terms British-Israelism or Anglo-Israelism do not appear in the book *The United States and British Commonwealth in Prophecy.* The author himself heard Garner Ted Armstrong a few years ago on a "World Tomorrow" broadcast shrug off the charge that he was preaching British-Israelism with a "whatever that is." Note carefully that this denial is not only consistent with the claim of prophetic uniqueness, but critical to it.

Understand Armstrong's position. He does not say, "I have examined British-Israelism and found it to be the key to understanding the Bible and am building upon it." He is affirming that he never heard of British-Israelism. He realizes that his message cannot be both a warmed-over British-Israelism and at the same time the true gospel that has not been preached for eighteen and one-half centuries. Therefore the mere existence of British-Israel theology for more than a century pre-Radio Church of God is a fatal embarrassment to Armstrong.

British-Israelism, also known variously as Anglo-Israelism and the Anglo-Saxon Federation, is an ideology that has as its central theme the identification of the Anglo-Saxon peoples as the true Israel and therefore heirs to all the promises in the Bible made by God to Israel. A man named Richard Brothers who lived in

18

England between 1757 and 1854 is credited with the origination of the system. Brothers was an eccentric who was eventually committed to an asylum.

It was John Wilson's *Our Israelitish Origin* (1840) that first clearly stated the theory as held today by British-Israel enthusiasts.[6]

The system sets out to prove that Israel came to occupy the British Isles by three different routes. First, a migration occurred as early as 1000 B.C. Later there was another with Jeremiah and Baruch and the princess Tamar Tephi, who wed King Eochaid, ruler of Ireland, himself descended from the earlier Israelite migration. The descendants of this royal line hold in trust the throne of England—which is the throne of David—for Christ who will return and occupy it. The last migration was that of the ten lost tribes of Israel which, after many generations of wandering, entered Britain as the Celts, Jutes, Danes, and Anglo-Saxons.

There is a very simple way in which the reader can determine for himself whether or not Armstrongism is, at its core, old British-Israelism. Read *The United States and British Commonwealth in Prophecy*. Then go to the library and read one of the standard British-Israel texts such as *Judah's Sceptre and Joseph's Birthright*, by J. H. Allen.[7] Allen's work was first published in 1902. Except for arrangement of material and the doctrine by Armstrong on the Law and the Sabbath and his modern predictions, you will find you are reading the same book. Foundational Armstrongism and British-Israelism are not similar—they are identical. In fact, it is the distinct impression of the author that the work by Allen is the primary source for *The United States and British*

[6] Charles S. Braden, "Anglo-Israel," *Twentieth Century Encyclopedia of Religious Knowledge* (Grand Rapids: Baker Book House, 1955), I, 44.

[7] J. H. Allen, *Judah's Sceptre and Joseph's Birthright* (Boston: A. A. Beauchamp, 1930).

Commonwealth in Prophecy. Read the introduction to the latter book where Armstrong affirms:

> And WHY have these prophecies not been understood or believed?
>
> Because the vital KEY that unlocks prophecy to our understanding has been lost. That KEY is the IDENTITY of the UNITED STATES and the BRITISH PEOPLES in Biblical prophecy.[8]

And then read the first paragraph in Chapter 6 of Allen's book:

> The very understanding of this difference is the KEY by which almost the entire Bible becomes intelligible, and I cannot state too strongly that the man who has not yet seen that Israel of Scripture is totally distinct from the Jewish people, is yet in the very infancy, the mere alphabet, of Biblical study, and that to this day the meaning of seven-eighths of the Bible is shut to his understanding.[9]

While reading Allen, you have to stop and check the book cover to assure yourself that you are not reading Armstrong.

So far from being lost, the British-Israel theory was a cultural myth of the British Empire. The literary chronicler of Victorian England, Rudyard Kipling, in the short story "The Man Who Would Be King," has two Englishmen working their way into the confidence of a tribe of remote Afghanistan to remodel it into an English monarchy over which they would rule. Says one of the men:

> I won't make a Nation, I'll make an Empire! These men aren't niggers; they're English! Look at their eyes—look at their mouths. Look at the way they stand up. They sit on chairs in their

8 Armstrong, *op. cit.,* p. xii.
9 Allen, *op. cit.,* p. 79.

20

own houses. They're the Lost Tribes, or something like it, and they've grown to be English.[10]

British-Israel theory has been bed-partner to various other religious theories. The methodology has logically permitted such alien and remote doctrines as pyramidology, [11] a racism that relegates all non-Anglos to the kingdom of the "beast of the field"[12] (Armstrong holds for strict racial segregation), and the most blatant political imperialism.[13]

British-Israelism is a theological sponge. Its methodology, not being seriously encumbered by facts, renders it so flexible that when evidence becomes obvious which seems to refute or embarrass it, it simply exercises its syncretistic system, absorbs the contrary evidence, and declares that both are true. A system that regularly harmonizes antipodes cannot be a reliable guide to truth. As the man who, every morning, mounted his horse and rode off in all directions, British-Israel adherents, in the name of truth and orthodoxy, have applied the fundamentals of the theory and galloped to every point on the ideological compass as if there were no other direction for a thinking person to take.

For example, in its original expressions, British-Israelism offered itself as the only reasonable fulfillment of Old Testament prophecy in general and the crucial deathbed promises of Jacob in particular. All of the dusty British-Israel volumes explain that the basic pro-

[10] John Beecroft (ed.), *Kipling, A Selection of His Stories and Poems* (New York: Doubleday & Co., Inc., 1956), p. 133.

[11] F. Haberman, *The Message of the Great Pyramid to the Anglo-Saxons* (St. Petersburg, Fla.: The Kingdom Press, 1928).

[12] *In the Image of God* (no author given) (Merrimac, Mass.: Destiny Publishers, 1967).

[13] Martin Lyman Streator, *The Anglo-American Alliance in Prophecy* (New Haven, Conn.: Our Race Pub. Co., 1900).

phetic justification for the theory is seen in the predictions made by the dying patriarch (Gen. 48). Jacob crosses his hands as he blesses the sons of Joseph. The greater blessing falls to Ephraim instead of first-born Manasseh. Manasseh was to become a nation, but the younger brother would be a greater one. It sounded respectable to affirm that the Anglo-Saxon peoples were "lost Israel" in general, and that Great Britain was Ephraim in particular and the United States Manasseh, when Great Britain was a mighty empire and the U.S. only a second-rate nation.

For a long time the movement of Western history favored the British-Israel interpretation of it. British-Israelism enjoyed its heyday in Victorian England. When Britannia ruled the waves, the theory thrived. The glory of the British Empire was the social context from which sprung the British-Israel interpretation of history full blown. The ascendancy of Ephraim was manifest. God was making no secret as to how He was keeping His promise to Abraham in the descendants of Israel.

But now that the sun daily sets on the British Empire and Ephraim has stood for a generation in the shadow of Manasseh, the theory is less tenable. Traditional British-Israelism demonstrated how the Scriptures unquestionably proved that the glory of British-Israel would continue to grow until the return of Jesus. At the moment of victory, the occupant of the throne of England, that is, the throne of David, would relinquish it to Christ and He would reign over the prepared kingdom and the restoration of Israel would be complete. But with the passing of time the empire-kingdom crumbled, the throne of England became a quaint anachronism preserved for the sake of nostalgia, prophecy after prophecy failed, and old British-Israelism all but died. The British-Israel motif was weighed, found wanting, and, for the most part, discreetly put aside.

Armstrong has juggled the basic British-Israel theory to hold that the Scriptures really show that it is *Manas-*

seh who was to become "the world's greatest single nation" after all. A system of Biblical interpretation that permits a foundational proposition to be reversed and the opposite proved, when vicissitudes require such a reversal, is as suspect as it is convenient.

USBCP[14] was copyrighted in 1967. Armstrong's romantic identification of lost Israel is greeted by many with the breathless wonder of a child on the imaginary trail of buried treasure. Earlier in the century it would have been greeted with a collective yawn. It would have been recognized as discredited British-Israelism.

The reason that most Americans have never heard of British-Israelism is that the key was quietly retired when the purported truth it unlocked proved to be historical foolishness. The survival of the claim of a lost key depends on popular ignorance of British-Israelism.

British-Israelism is not the private domain of Armstrongism even today. In England, South Africa, Canada, and to a lesser degree in the United States there survive vestiges of the system. A list of diehards still holding for the theory includes Destiny Publishers, Merrimac, Massachusetts; Canadian British-Israel Association, Ottawa, Ontario; The Covenant Publishing Co., London; National Forecast Publications, Topton, North Carolina; The Federation of the Covenant People, Johannesburg, South Africa; and British-Israel-World Federation (Canada), Inc., Toronto, Ontario.

"The World Tomorrow" program is the heir to such radio ministries as that of Dr. John Matthews, the "Shepherd of the Air." This broadcast flourished on the Pacific coast from British Columbia to California in the 1930s. Herbert W. Armstrong began to preach British-Israelism in Eugene, Oregon, January, 1934. James Lovell of Fort Worth, Texas, preached the system on as many as sixty stations in Canada and the United States.

---

14 Shortened form for *The United States and British Commonwealth in Prophecy* will be used from now on.

British-Israelism in the states was on the wane when Armstrong began his ministry. He did not publish his basic text, *USBCP*, until 1967.

Armstrongism, by definition and by admission, must deny any debt to traditional British-Israelism. Anyone who takes the time to read the historically discredited assertions of past British-Israel enthusiasts will not be impressed by the first chapter of *USBCP* where the discovery of the key is announced. He will be amused.

The presence of aging volumes on library shelves which are mirrors of *USBCP* stands as available and unanswerable proof that Herbert W. Armstrong and Company are false prophets.

In order to test the validity of this proposition, the author attended a "Bible lecture" held by Armstrongites. After the session he approached the speaker, a graduate of Ambassador College, a man who traveled about giving such lectures, and who must be considered a competent representative of the Armstrongite position. In response to questions he affirmed that the doctrine of the Worldwide Church of God as taught by Armstrong is "definitely from heaven." When asked about any connection with traditional British-Israelism, he responded, "Definitely not British-Israelism." When the author produced the book by Allen (of which the lecturer was aware), the lecturer reluctantly admitted that Armstrong could have been directed by God to read the "truth" in a book. The next question was as to how it could then be from heaven and not from men and in what way could it have been lost? No answer.

British-Israelism is the skeleton of Armstrongism. The proposition that Armstrongism is *not* British-Israelism is the heartbeat of Armstrongism. Take away both the skeleton and the heart, and Armstrongism stands as a conspicuous and ludicrous scarecrow.

2 THE "LOST TRIBES"

The pre-Armstrong existence of the "key" brands Armstrong a deceiver. It is herein demonstrated that the key (the identification of Anglo-Saxons as "Israel") does not open the Bible to human understanding anyway. Armstrongism requires the relocation of Israel from the northern real estate of Israel to the British Isles. British-Israelism—Armstrongism is a "Lost Tribes" theory. The eye-popping "identifications" made from fanciful and anachronistic Anglo-Saxon folklore, real or imagined, may be very appealing to the person given to religious fiction. But the romance fades when the full range of Lost Tribes identifications is surveyed. Armstrongism is only one of many Lost Tribes theories.

The Theory of the Lost Ten Tribes of Israel

The basic theory of Lost Israel has three thrusts:

1. All the inhabitants of the northern kingdom of Hoshea were deported by Shalmaneser and Sargon, 722-718 B.C.[1]

2. The House of Israel has never returned but is (or

---

[1] A parenthetical consideration concerning the deportation of the northern kingdom is the question of exactly which Assyrian ruler accomplished the feat, Shalmaneser or Sargon. According to the Assyrian record, the fall of Samaria took place in the ninth year of Hoshea; that is, 722-21 B.C. If this is so, Samaria must

has been) wandering among the nations, more or less intact as a people, unaware, for the most part, of its identity. It is waiting to emerge and have realized in it the restoration promises of the prophets.

3. The romantic search for Lost Israel is justified by the restoration and kingdom prophecies of the Old Testament. These have never been fulfilled, and hence the integrity of God anticipates and requires vindication.

Thus, according to the theory of Lost Israel, the people of the ten tribes who rebelled against Rehoboam were a total population in anonymous pilgrimage.

The Source of the Theory of the Lost Ten Tribes of Israel

The term "Lost Ten Tribes" does not appear in the Bible. The source is the mythical and apocryphal book of II Esdras. The author, impersonating the scribe Ezra, with whose canonical book there is no connection, wrote late in the first century A.D.[2] It is a collection of

have been taken before Nisan, 722 B.C. But Sargon came to the throne about nine months later. Hence, Sargon could not have captured Samaria at the beginning of his reign, as he claims. Josephus says that Shalmaneser was the conqueror of Samaria. It is clear that the fall of Samaria took place during that transitional period in which Shalmaneser died and Sargon succeeded him. No real problem exists. A reasonable explanation is offered by Edward J. Young in *The Book of Isaiah* (Grand Rapids: Eerdmans, 1965) on page 19: "On the other hand it is quite possible that Sargon may have been present at the fall of Samaria as a general rather than as king. He may in that sense have captured the city, as he himself states. What can be conclusively asserted is that the Scriptural account which attributes the capture of Shalmanezer is true to fact."

2 Critics generally believe that the eagle in the fifth vision of II Esdras (11:1; 12:51) represents the Roman Empire. The three heads of the eagle are thought to represent Vespasian, Titus, and Domitian. The destruc-

"apocalyptic" visions. It does not claim to be a historical narrative. The account goes:

> And whereas thou sawest that he gathered another peaceable multitude unto him; Those are the ten tribes, which were carried away prisoners out of their own land in the time of Osea the king, whom Salmanasar the king of Assyria led away captive, and he carried them over the waters, and so came they into another land. But they took counsel among themselves, that they would leave the multitude of the heathen, and go forth into a further country, where never mankind dwelt, That they might there keep their statutes, which they never kept in their own land. And they entered into Euphrates by the narrow passages of the river. For the most High then shewed signs for them, and held still the flood, till they were passed over. For through that country there was a great way to go, namely, of a year and a half: and the same region is called Arsareth[3]

Josephus, also writing late first century A.D., muddies the waters by placing the ten tribes at the very place from which the author of Esdras claims they had miraculously escaped.

> ... but then the entire body of the people of Israel remained in that country; wherefore there are but two tribes in Asia and Europe subject to the Romans, while the ten tribes are beyond Euphrates till now, and are an immense multitude, and not to be estimated by numbers.[4]

Indicative of the mythical nature of the theory is

tion of Jerusalem mentioned so frequently in the book is probably that by Titus in A.D. 70. The book of II Esdras must therefore date to the last quarter of the first century. See Kaufman Kohler, "Books of Esdras," in *Jewish Encyclopedia* (1906), V, 221.

[3] II Esdras 13:39-45.

[4] *Antiq.* XI. v. 2.

the confusion as to the location of the ten lost tribes. Josephus places them "beyond Euphrates" in the first century A.D., and Esdras has them gone from Euphrates to "another land." Armstrong says that Daniel, who was in the Mesopotamian area where "Israel" was taken, could not have dealt with them because they were "lost from view" and it was "as if the earth had opened her mouth and swallowed them!"[5] The confusion increases when we read Josephus at one time saying that the ten tribes were taken out of Samaria (*Antiq.* X. ix. 7), and at another time claiming that they were deported from "Judea" (*Antiq.* IX. xiv. 1).

There are at least two possible explanations for the inconsistencies. One, the prejudice of the Jews against the Samaritans. In the first century, it was axiomatic that the "Jews have no dealings with the Samaritans" (John 4:9). Josephus makes no attempt to conceal his contempt for the Samaritans. He accuses them of affirming Israelite ancestry when profitable and convenient, and denying it when things are going badly for the Jews (*Antiq.* XI. viii. 6). Having ten-tribed Israel beyond Euphrates would justify the contempt the Jew could feel toward the purely "Gentile" Samaritan. Having Israel absent may have been, for Josephus, more emotional than historical.

The second and more probable explanation is the understanding of what the first-century Jews actually meant when they used the terms "ten tribes" and "two tribes." Josephus may be unconsciously showing the first-century concept of these distinctions. All knew that the two tribes were carried away into Babylon in the same sense that the ten tribes were carried to Assyria. (The account in II Kings 17 of the deportation does not use the term "ten tribes.") The careless use of the terms by Josephus may reflect the fact that the mutually exclusive terminology did not distinguish specific tribes

5 *USBCP*, p. 7.

from other specific tribes at all. The popular speech probably indicated nothing more than the distinction between majority Eastern or Babylonian Judaism and minority Western Judaism of the Roman Empire. He expected his readers to understand. They did not consider any tribes to be lost.

The author of II Esdras is writing in the time of Domitian. Jerusalem is gone. The Jewish state is dissolved. Babylonian Judaism is the last hope for the restoration. Arabian raiders are threatening the eastern segment of Judaism. The ten tribes must escape. The book of II Esdras is the fanciful tale of how the ten tribes are supernaturally led into seclusion until the storm should pass.[6]

Other Identifications of Lost Israel

Armstrong announces that "the whereabouts of the Lost Ten Tribes is one of the ancient mysteries *now cleared up!*" Before we fall all over ourselves in gratitude that a mystery (of which many have probably never heard before) is now solved, we ought to survey the claims of many other detective-prophets who have made the same assertion. Armstrong is simply the most recent of a long line of Lost Tribes hunters who have claimed the distinction of being discoverer of "Israel."

Contending with the Worldwide Church of God for the copyright on Lost Israel is the Church of Jesus Christ of Latter-Day Saints (Mormon). The Book of Mormon claims to be "an abridgment of the record of the people of Nephi and also of the Lamanites written to the Lamanites, who are a remnant of the house of Israel."[7] According to the Mormon Church, the Lamanites,

[6] See Allen H. Godbey, *The Lost Tribes a Myth* (Durham, N.C.: Duke University Press, 1930).

[7] Joseph Smith (trans.), Book of Mormon (Salt Lake City: Church of Jesus Christ of Latter-Day Saints, 1950), title page.

cursed with dark skin because of the wickedness of that people in slaughtering the righteous Nephites, are Lost Israel and the ancestors of the American Indian. It is not necessary to go into the story of how and why a remnant of Israel arrived in the New World.

In the early 1800s near Palmyra, New York, Smith claimed to have had a midnight visit from the angel Moroni who told him where to find the plates buried by the last of the Nephites. Modern Mormons make the same claim as Armstrongites—the identity of Lost Israel was a revelation from God.

Joseph Smith did not need a midnight visitor to show him gold plates which would advise him of the true identity of the American Indian. As British-Israelism was in England, so this theory was a cultural myth of colonial America. The theory began as a theological proposition, not an ethnological one. It apparently originated with Joannes Fredericus Lumnius in his work *De Extremo Dei Indicio et Indorum Vocatione* published at Antwerp in 1567.[8] Lumnius did not exhaustively examine the American aboriginal cultures. The basis for his version of how the House of Israel arrived in the New World was the Book of Esdras. Lumnius did not consider Esdras to be apocryphal. The reasoning of Lumnius was probably thus: Since the Lost Tribes have to be somewhere, and they have not been satisfactorily identified anwhere else, the newly discovered American native is the only live possibility.

When the white European found the New World Indian, he naturally pondered his racial origin. The theory of the Lost Ten Tribes was the handiest and most attractive working hypothesis. Christopher Columbus thought himself to be not only the discoverer of a new land, but also of Lost Israel.[9] His conclusion was based on his study of Esdras.

8 Lee Eldridge Huddleston, *Origins of the American Indians* (Austin: University of Texas Press, 1967), p. 34.

9 Back in Lisbon, Columbus read assiduously in Car-

The identification of the New World peoples as Lost Israel took shape in the eighteenth century when Lord Kingsborough[10] and others thought they saw in the Mexican culture traces of Israelite culture. The early Mormon movement did not have exclusive rights on the theory. No less an educator than Samuel Sewall[11] of Harvard and no less a religious leader than Jonathan Edwards[12] shared the view.

Kingsborough listed seventeen principal reasons for the identification of the American Indians as Lost Israel. The identifications parallel the kind of thing Armstrong presents as evidence of the British-Israel identification. Kingsborough "observed" that the Indians had some knowledge of God, practiced circumcision on occasion, expected a Messiah, used words that seemed to be of Hebrew or Greek derivation, had rites and ceremonies that bore resemblance to Hebrew ritual, imitated Hebrew moral laws, and had paintings bearing "traces of Jewish superstitions, history, traditions, laws, manners, and customs."[13] As in the case of Columbus, Kingsborough indicated that the seed of his conclusion had been planted by the Book of Esdras.

dinal Pierre d'Ailly's *Image of the World* and Marco Polo's account of the East. But though he studied Ptolemy and certainly knew Toscanelli's opinion, the system of ideas he elaborated owed most to "the prophet" Esdras (Salvador de Madariaga, "Christopher Columbus," *Encyclopaedia Britannica* [31st ed.], VI, 111).

[10] Lord Kingsborough, *Antiquities of Mexico* (London: Robert Havell & Colnaghi, Son, & Co., 1831), VI, 113.

[11] Samuel Sewall, *Some Few Lines Towards a Description of the New Heaven as it makes to those who stand upon the New Earth* (Boston: printed by Bartholomew Green and sold by Benjamin Eliot, Samuel Gerrish & Daniel Henchman, 1727), p. A.

[12] Jonathan Edwards, *Observations on the Language of the Muhhekaneew Indians* (New York: M. L. & W. A. Davis, 1801), p. 5.

[13] Kingsborough, *op. cit.*, pp. 113-116.

Jonathan Edwards, as a youth, became proficient in the language of the Muhhekaneew Indians by playing with Indian neighbors. He saw in the language traces of Hebrew.

Charles Crawford, writing late in the eighteenth century, concluded that the "aborigines of America were probably the descendants of Noah" and that America afterwards was "further peopled by the Ten Tribes, who were taken captive by Shalmaneser, king of Assyria." He cites Esdras and concludes that not all the ten tribes came to the New World, but that "it is probable that a part of the Ten Tribes remained in the country, where they were carried near Habor (which is now called Tabor)."[14]

Other Identifications

In the high mountains of the Szechwan Province of China near the Tibetan border dwells a race of worshipers who have no link with ancient Far Eastern Judaism, but who have been tagged Lost Israel.[15] About 1915 a missionary named Torrance so identified the people on the basis of the following identifications: (a) monotheism (later proved to be nonexistent); (b) flat-roofed houses; (c) marriage of a widow to the brother of her deceased husband; (d) sacrifice of a "lamb" (actually a grown goat); and (e) certain similarities in words.

The aforementioned fictional identification by Kipling of Afghan clans as Lost Israel was based on a popular notion of his day. The Afghans themselves have

14 *An Essay on the Propagation of the Gospel in Which There Are Numerous Facts and Arguments Adduced to prove that many of the Indians In America Are descended from the Ten Tribes* (Philadelphia: James Humphreys, 1801), p. 7.

15 David Crockett Graham, *The Customs and Religion of the Ch'iang* (Washington, D.C.: Smithsonian Institute, 1958), 135[1], 96-98.

a tradition that they are descendants of the lost Ten Tribes. In a native book *Tabakati-Nasiri*, it is stated that at the time of the Shansabi dynasty, there was a people called Bani Israel. These "sons of Israel" were supposed to have been converted to Islam about the year 622. This throws no light, however, upon the source of the modern Jews of Afghanistan.[16]

The Karens of Burma, numbering over a million and living in Eastern and Southern Burma, are of a racial origin that seems to be dissimilar, at least in part, to the Burmese in general. They have been put forward as candidates for the title Lost Israel, the following points of identification offered as evidence: (a) Jewish appearance, (b) the name used for God ("Ywwah"), and (c) the use of bones of fowls for divination purposes.

A Japanese sect, the Shindai, have been labeled Lost Israel in a book by N. McLeod.[17] The Shindai or holy class of Japan were seen as descendants of the Samarian deportees with the following similarities cited:

1. The first known king in Japan was Osee, 730 B.C., and the last king of Israel was Hosea, who died 722 B.C.

2. The Shinto temple is divided into a holy place and a most holy place.

3. The priests wear a linen dress bonnet, and breeches like the Jewish priests of old.

4. Ancient worship of the Shindai seems to be connected with patriarchal Israelite worship.

5. Ancient temple instruments are used in the Shinto temple.

6. The Shindai have "Jewish appearance."

The Karaites of Russia, a heretical Jewish sect founded in Bagdad about A.D. 765, comes forward as a

[16] Joseph Jacobs, "Afghanistan," *Jewish Encyclopedia*, I, 223.

[17] *Epitome of the Ancient History of Japan* (Tokyo, 1879).

claimant of the title Lost Israel. Their reputation as a part of the Lost Tribes is the result of certain claims made from within the clan. In order to avoid the persecution being directed toward Rabbinate Jews, the Karaites attempted to prove they were guiltless of the execution of Jesus because they were descended from the lost Ten Tribes and had been settled in the Crimea since the time of Shalmaneser.[18]

The Hindus, a significant segment of the population of the world, have been labeled Lost Israel. Attempts have been made to prove that the high-class Hindus, including all the Buddhists, are descendants of the Scythians, who were the Lost Ten Tribes. (Here there is common ground with British-Israelism—Armstrongism.) Buddhism is set forth as a fraudulent development of Old Testament doctrines brought to India by the Ten Tribes.[19]

In 1835 Asahel Grant, an American physician, was appointed by the American Board of Foreign Missions to pursue his calling among the Nestorians of Mesopotamia. He found among them a tradition that they were descendants of the Lost Ten Tribes. The points of identification were: (a) they were "beyond Euphrates" where Josephus had located the Ten Tribes; (b) language, a branch of the Aramaic; (c) the offering of sacrifices and first-fruits; (d) preparation for the Sabbath on the preceding evening; and (e) Jewish names and features. Grant also held that the Yezidis, or devil-worshipers, of the same area were descended from Lost Israel. They observed the rite of circumcision, offered sacrifices, including that of the paschal lamb on the 24th of Nisan, and abstained from forbidden food.[20]

On the basis of similarity of customs, appearance or

18 Joseph Jacobs, "Lost Ten Tribes," *Jewish Encyclopedia*, XII, 249.
19 *Ibid.*
20 *Ibid.*

physiognomy, traditions, and other traces of "Hebrew" culture, the following have been identified more or less seriously as the deported tribes of the northern kingdom:

1. Abkhasians of the Caucasus.
2. Abyssinian aborigines.
3. Bahutsim Jews of North Africa.
4. Brazil Jews of the West Indies.
5. Cabinda Negroes of Loango Coast.
6. Chalybes, a people of Armenia.
7. Daghestanians of the Armenian Mountains.
8. Masai or Mazai, Hamitic people of East Africa.
9. Ephthalites of the area beyond the Aral Sea.
10. Habr-tribes of Somaliland.
11. Kamants of Abyssinia.
12. Kaffirs of South Africa.
13. Zulus, so identified by a Dr. Tyler, forty years a Congregational missionary.
14. Tartars, called Lost Israel by Arron Hill of London, 1709.
15. Ambaka Negroes, called Lost Israel by David Livingstone.
16. Melkites, Arab Christians.
17. Me'unim people of Ma'on, Arabia.
18. Mingrelians, at the east end of the Black Sea.
19. Moussai, "Moses-folk" of Persia and Turkestan.
20. Nupes of Nigeria.
21. Sindians, tribes along the north side of the Black Sea, east of the Crimea.
22. Subbotniki, "Sabbath people," partially Judaized Russians.
23. Tebu, Tibesti, Negroids of eastern Sahara.
24. Troglodyte Jews of Tripoli and Tunis.
25. Uzbecks or Uzbegs, a Turkoman tribe.
26. Wakalindi of East Africa.
27. Zadokites of Damascus.

When British-Israelism—Armstrongism boldly asserts that the Anglo-Saxons are Lost Israel, the temptation is to respond, "Who isn't?" If all the national groups that have been candidates for the office of the lost Ten Tribes were removed from the world, hardly enough would remain to make up a crew for Noah's ark. As for identifying marks pointing to Israelite descent, there is an embarrassment of riches.

The universality of identification does not *ipso facto* disprove the particular identification of British-Israelism—Armstrongism. The presence of universal identifications logically forces Armstrong, however, either to offer supporting evidence for his identification from alternate disciplines, or to admit that his identification is simply one of many others of the same kind.

The plethora of identifications places upon Armstrong the burden of proving that his identification is unique and actually points to Israelite descent, whereas all other identifications are imagined, forced, or a matter of coincidence. He must show that his points of similarity indicate a connection with the deported northern kingdom and that all others necessarily have alternative explanations. If Armstrong cannot demonstrate that British-Israel identifications are qualitatively superior to the others, the arguments he offers from early European tradition and legend are inconclusive.

Sources of Traditions of Israelite Descent and Traces of Hebrew Culture

The preceding section surveyed the national groups that have vied for the title Lost Israel. The error of tracing every piece of ethnological evidence that has a Hebrew scent about it back to the deportation of Israel by Shalmaneser is demonstrated in this section.

The deportation of Israelites from Samaria by the Assyrian monarch was only one of many such deportations. Some were larger, some were smaller. Deportation did not begin with the imperial policy of Assyria in the seventh century B.C. The exporting of sections of the

36

populace began with early Israelite defeats and continued throughout the Roman wars. The spread of the
historically vigorous Hebrew culture has been via many
avenues. The enthusiam of the Jews for proselyting has
contributed to the spread of culture patterns characteris-
tically Hebrew. The forced promiscuity that attends all
wars has added to the stream of Jewishness which
flowed into the "nations." The dispersion of Israelites
has been a monotonous theme of history. The Jew is
Chinese and yellow, is African and black, is Nordic and
white, and every shade in between. No "race" exists.
Each expression of Judaism sees itself as ancient as that
of the Mediterranean Jew. When the whole picture is
seen, one will not be surprised to discover traces of what
appear to be vestiges of the Israelite culture, but rather
not to find traces in any given part of the world.

We are not lending to these British-Israelism—Armstrongism claims of the discovery of Israel in the British
Isles the respectability of dealing with them as history.
However, this section presents alternatives to the Lost
Israel motif as possible explanations for any germ of fact
that might be present in the various Lost Tribes recon-
structions of the histories of ethnic sources.

Other Deportations

If British-Israelism—Armstrongism could produce a
nation of Anglo-Saxons with "Israelite" stamped on
their foreheads, this would not necessarily identify them
as the lost Ten Tribes of Israel. To argue for the Lost
Tribes theory by citing traditions of descent from Israelite wanderings is to make certain presuppositions, mostly
unwarranted. It is to presuppose the total deportation
and national or racial survival of the northern kingdom
of Hoshea. It is to presuppose that there were no other
dispersions of Hebrews from whom later resemblances to
Judaism might arise. It is to assume that the conditions
of life in the new homes of the exiles could not have

favored the spread of Judaism there. It is to ignore other avenues of the dissemination of Hebrew culture. It is demonstrated here that the Samarian deportees of 722-721 B.C. were not the main bloc of Israelitish peoples shifted about in the ancient Near East.

Every war in which ancient Israel was worsted meant exile for many. The account of the 32,000 captive Midianite maidens (Num. 31:35) gives an indication of what Israel might expect when the tables were turned. It is not necessary to give a complete list of defeats in the early part of the history of Israel. This point is established by observing the lengthy war in which Damascus reduced the northern kingdom drastically (II Kings 13:1-8). The dispersion of Israelite captives through Aramaean lands, and through lands where Israelite captives were sold (Amos 1:9) spread the influence of that people. Also Aramaean garrisons and settlers in defeated Israel produced national intermingling (I Kings 20:34).

A century before the forays of Nebuchadrezzar into Judah, Sennacherib reports the deportation of 200,150 from southwest Judah.[21] This is at least six times as many as Shalmaneser and Sargon removed from Samaria twenty years earlier.

Nebuchadrezzar deported thousands from the southern kingdom. Jeremiah lists 4,600 (52:28-30). Ten thousand or more of the nation's best were later put on the road to Babylon.

In the seventh and sixth centuries B.C. the Egyptian kings Psamtik I and II (Gr., Psammetichus), of the twenty-sixth or Saite Dynasty, carried away large bodies of Jews, and, according to Josephus, placed them as garrisons on the Nubian frontier.[22] Aristeas does not estimate the number, but records that:

[21] D. Winton Thomas, *Documents from Old Testament Times* (New York: Harper & Row, 1961), p. 67.

[22] *Antiq.* XII. i. 1; XII. ii. 5.

Many Jews had already before this entered the country along with the Persians, and others had at a still earlier time been sent out as auxiliaries to fight in the army of Psammetichus against the king of the Ethiopians; but these immigrants were not so large a body as those whom Ptolemy, son of Lagus, introduced.[23]

Both Aristeas and Josephus give accounts of the conquest of Coele-Syria and the deportation of at least 100,000 Jews by Ptolemy Soter.[24] Josephus puts the number taken captive at 120,000.[25] Aristeas also tells how the Persian Cambyses had previously encouraged the settlement of Jews in Egypt.[26]

History records the deportation of thousands of Jews in the wars that followed the campaigns of Ptolemy Soter. In the Maccabean wars several thousands became exiles. Herodian wars and Parthinian raids meant the same.[27] Ptolemy Lathyrus, first century B.C., deported 100,000 Jewish slaves from Galilee, more from the battle on the Jordan, and still more in subsequent mopping-up actions.[28] Following the slaughter, the reports of which vary from thirty to fifty thousand, "as for the rest, they were part of them taken captives, and the other part ran away to their own country."[29]

The Roman general Crassus captured many at the battle of Taricheae. Josephus claims "he went up into Judea also, and fell upon Taricheae and presently took it, and carried about thirty thousand Jews captive."[30]

[23] Letter of Aristeas 13. (Aristeas, although commonly viewed as apocryphal, reflects a reasonably accurate picture of this general history.)

[24] Arist. l. 12-13; 35-37. *Antiq.* XII. ii. 5.

[25] *Antiq.* XII. ii. 3.

[26] Arist. l. 13.

[27] *Antiq.* XIV. xii. 1-9.

[28] *Ibid.*, XIII. xii. 4.

[29] *Ibid.*, XIII. xii. 5.

[30] *Ibid.*, XIV. vii. 3.

In His prediction about the fall of Jerusalem (which occurred A.D. 70, Jesus warned that it would be a terrible time for the Jews in and about the city and that the siege would end with them being "led away captive into all nations" (Luke 21:24). The clashes of races and religions in Syria and Palestine eventually brought Vespasian and Titus. They stormed Jewish communities, massacred and enslaved thousands. The recurring tragedy was that "their cities were taken by force, and their wives and children carried into slavery."[31]

Allowing for the distortion of statistics, it is the inevitable conclusion that the Samarian deportation was merely one such national catastrophe among many others, most of which were much larger. If God had led prophets of the stature of Jeremiah and Isaiah to emphasize and dramatize these other defeats and deportations in the same way as they did the fall of Samaria and the deportation of "Israel," then they would have loomed as large in history. Those carried captive by Shalmaneser and Sargon were a very small fraction—probably not 1 percent—of the total number seized and deported by various peoples during many centuries.

Proselytes

Deportations were far from being the only avenue of the dissemination of Israelitish culture. The common accusation that Jews have not been evangelistic does not necessarily hold true for much of their history. The Law of Moses required religious exclusiveness. It did not require national segregation and it did not discourage proselyting. The ruthless repression of Jewish proselyting by European and Moslem governments through a century and a half has produced a reluctance to evangelize which has so often been misrepresented as indifference to missionary effort. This reluctance to proselyte has been accepted as a definitive characteristic of Juda-

31 Josephus, *Life*, 16.

ism, but it has been projected too far into the past. Active proselyting may have been as large a factor as deportations in the spreading of the Hebrew religio-culture.

Before there can be an election of race, as Lost Tribes hunters normally claim, there must be an identifiable race. A study of the original Theocracy shows that the idea of an Israelite or Jewish "race" has been a myth from the beginning. Yahweh worshipers of "Gentile" races or those of the "nations" repeatedly appear in the Old Testament (e.g., Ruth and Rahab). The Book of Esther records that "many of the people of the land became Jews; for the fear of the Jews fell upon them" (8:17). These converts were included in the agreement producing the institution of Purim (9:27). Isaiah rebuked prejudice expressed toward Judaized "strangers" (56:3), and commanded that those who had covenanted to follow Yahweh were to have equal privileges in worship (vv. 6-8).

Constant proselyting was such a universal practice in ancient Israel that it is a feature even of the restoration promises of the prophets (Isa. 14:1). In the new heavens and new earth promise of Isaiah 66, the Gentiles are to be made priests and Levites (v. 21).

Approaching the Christian era, the evidence is of enthusiastic proselyting. Jesus recognized that the scribes and Pharisees circled "sea and land to make one proselyte" (Matt. 23:15). The Book of Acts is a study of the Christian witness to Jewish proselyte communities.

In the Talmud, full proselytes are declared to hold an inferior position in the Jewish community, but may intermarry with all social grades, except the priestly (*Kiddushin* 4).

According to Josephus, the people of both Greek and barbarian cities displayed a great zeal for the Jewish religion. He argues that the Jewish culture had permeated all areas of the empire during the two decades after the fall of Jerusalem:

41

Nay, further, the multitudes of mankind itself have had a great inclination of a long time, to
follow our religious observances; for there is not
any city of the Grecians, nor any of the barbari-
ans, nor any nation whatsoever whither our custom of resting on the seventh day hath not
come.[32]

It is stretching the term proselyte to use it to
describe the manner in which Hyrcanus dealt with the
defeated people of Syria after the death of Antiochus.
He permitted the Idumeans to stay in that country only
if they would submit to circumcision and agree to adopt
the laws of the Jews.[33] They agreed and were "Jewish"
throughout their subsequent history.[34]

Philo and the Alexandrian sages continued in the
spirit of Isaiah, Habakkuk, and Jeremiah, exposing the
perversion and intellectual paucity of heathen religions.
During the last ten years that preceded the destruction
of the Judaean State, there were more proselytes than
there had been at any other time. Philo relates from his
own experience that in his native country many heathens, embracing Judaism, changed their lives and became
conspicuous by the practice of Hebrew virtue.[35]

Tacitus joins Cicero,[36] Juvenal,[37] Horace,[38] and
Seneca[39] in expressing irritation and disgust (shared by
most Romans) at seeing vast numbers of Greeks and
Romans proselyted to what they considered a hateful
superstition. He records that at one time the Senate
decreed that four thousand adult ex-slaves who had been

32 *Contra Apion* II. 40.
33 *Antiq.* XII. ix. 1. See also XIII. xi. 3.
34 *Ibid.*, XIV. viii. 1; XV. vii. 9; *Wars* II. iii. 1; IV. iv. 5
35 *De Virtutibus*, l. 182.
36 *Pro Flacco*, l. 18, 28.
37 *Juvenal* XIV. 96.
38 *Satires* I. lx. 69; IV. 142.
39 *De Superstitione.*

"tainted" with those superstitions should be transported to Sardinia to suppress banditry there, in the hope that the unhealthy climate would kill them.[40]

The record is clear that wherever Jews went, for any reason and under any circumstance, the Jewish cultural patterns were passed on to the surrounding pagan community. Many would imitate parts of the Hebrew culture. Many became full-fledged proselytes. Paganism had nothing that could withstand the elevated theology of the religion of the Jews, and had no culture of its own with the innate strength of Judaism.

The consideration of both deportation and occupation by alien armies introduces the fact of forced promiscuity. Wars, deportations, raids, exceptional oppression—these have always meant the violation of the women. As the nation of Israel gathered on Gerizim and Ebal to rehearse alternately the blessings and curses of keeping or breaking the Law, this warning was included: "Thou shalt betroth a wife, and another man shall lie with her" (Deut. 28:30).

The women of the ancient Near East were the inevitable spoils of war. The women of no other nation have been more abused than those of Israel. The children of such unholy alliances would almost invariably be raised Jewish. It was the uncommon thing for the father to take an interest in the training of the child. Often the father would have no further contact with his victim. The captivities of Israel, from the earliest, have done very little to squelch the determined spirit of the Jewish mother to bring up her child in the culture and religion of that people. Witness the training of Moses.

The song of Miriam has the approaching Egyptian charioteers boast, "My lust shall be satisfied upon them" (Exod. 15:9). In the song of Deborah, the women of the house of Sisera express the confidence, "Have they not divided the prey; to every man a damsel or two?"

---

[40] *Annals* II. 85 f.

(Judg. 5:30). As Israel and Judah fell to their enemies from the east, a regular feature of the lamentation was that for the fate of the women:

> Mine eye affecteth mine heart because of all the daughters of my city (Lam. 3:51).

> ... their houses shall be spoiled, and their wives ravished (Isa. 13:16).

> Therefore thus saith the Lord: Thy wife shall be an harlot in the city, and thy sons and thy daughters shall fall by the sword (Amos 7:17).

In the Maccabean wars the rape of Jewish women continued.

The Jews of Germany are the descendants of such tragedy. The Frankish Jews, and those that lived in Austria, descend from the time when the Vangioni had chosen from the vast horde of Jewish prisoners the most beautiful women. They brought them back to their stations on the shores of the Rhine and the Main, and compelled them to minister to the satisfaction of their desires. The children thus begotten were brought up by their mothers in the Jewish religion. These children come-of-age are said to have been the founders of the first Jewish communities between Worms and Mayence.[41]

In the Talmud a certain Judah Ben Ezekiel, Babylonian Amora of the second generation (*ca.* 220-299), was very concerned about the purity of the race. He was so particular on this point that he delayed marrying his son Isaac long after the boy had reached maturity, because he was not certain whether the family from which he desired to procure a wife was spotless beyond all dispute. His friend Ulla rebuked him, reminding him that Judah himself could not have proved that he was

---

41 Heinrich Graetz, *History of the Jews* (Philadelphia: The Jewish Publ. Soc. of America, 1956), III, 40 f.

not an offspring from the heathens who violated the maidens at the siege of Jerusalem.[42]

Add to this the women appropriated by the soldiers of Jewish garrisons. The soldiers released by Ptolemy Philadelphus, for instance, claimed the women they had taken as part of their pay.[43]

Dispersion

For most of its history, Judaism has been a religio-culture without benefit of real estate. As the people of Hebrew origin and tradition have moved, they have taken root at various places and grown a new strain of "Jewishness." It should be hard *not* to find traces of Hebrew culture since it is hard not to find Jews infiltrating almost every culture almost everywhere in almost every generation. The second chapter of Acts lists seventeen areas from which Jews came to celebrate Pentecost. In most of these places the Jews remained a minority culture, a religious enclave. The vigor and tenacity of Judaism has often allowed it to survive the passing of the cultures in which it has been submerged, and in some cases to become dominant within certain boundaries. These brands of local Judaism date from the earliest times. Some of them are so venerable that their beginning is lost in time and tradition.

European Jewry is self-evident beyond the need for more than passing mention. Less well known, but equally durable, are the expressions of Judaism listed next.

There are the Yemen Jews. The tradition among Yemen Jews of the southwestern part of Arabia is that their forefathers settled there forty-two years before the destruction of the first Temple. Modern Jewish ethnologists believe that the actual immigration of Jews into Yemen appears to have taken place about the beginning of the second Christian century.

[42] *Kiddushin* 4, 71 b.
[43] Arist. l. 14.

The origin of the Falasha ("Emigrant") Jews of Abyssinia is unknown. There is a tradition that they left Jerusalem in the retinue of Menilek, the son of Solomon and the Queen of Sheba. Others believe that Falashas to have been the prisoners of Shalmaneser, or of Jews driven from Judea when Jerusalem was destroyed at the time of Titus and Vespasian.

The Berber Jews, an indigenous, Caucasoid peoples of North Africa, along with the Negroes of that area, are outside the Berber social structure. The remarkable thing about this group is the presence of Palestinian traditions. The durability of these traditions is testimony to the assimilative energy of the Hebrew-Phoenician culture in North Africa.

Then there are the Black Jews of India. In the province of Bombay there are "Bene-Israel" who follow the Sephardic ritual and observe dietary laws. According to their own tradition, the original company of Jews landed on the western coast of India about the fourth or sixth century A.D. There is little doubt that proselytes in large numbers joined the original community, chiefly through slavery and polygamy. In appearance the Bene-Israel differ little from their Hindu neighbors.

There is a Negro Judaism that neither apologizes to other expressions of Judaism for its existence nor acknowledges any as parent. Rabbi Haling Hank Lenht (also named Bishop A. W. Cook, of Montclair, New Jersey), has declared that the Negroes are the only real Hebrews. Negro chieftains of the Gold Coast wear robes with Arabic and Hebrew charms. People of the Moorish Zionist Temple in New York claim as ancestors three Jewish tribes driven into Africa by civil wars among the ancient Hebrews. Numerous isolated tribes in Africa exhibit forms of "Jewishness."

The ancient caravan routes carried more than silk and spices to China. The Chinese Jews are pure Mongolians—Chinese in dress, language, habits, customs, in everything but religion. The eastward spread of Judaism

46

is evidenced by the Babylonian Talmud, which recognizes the necessity of the Scriptures in the cuneiform Assyrian, Elamite, Median, and Persian languages, as well as the Aramaic.[44] Genghis Khan had a corps of Jewish Mongol troops. He invited Jews driven from Samarcand and Bokhara into Persia to return, but he fanatically stamped out Christian churches in Tartary and Turkestan. Chinese Judaism suffered at the hands of the Moslems, but the culture has been as tenacious there as in other parts of the world.

Judaism certainly reached Japan. In the province of Yamato are two ancient villages called Goshen and Menashe (Manasseh). No Japanese etymology exists for these names. The legend is that in the third century of the Christian era a strange people, numbering about one hundred, appeared. A temple known as the Tent of David still stands where they first settled. A legend says that the founder of the sect, when a child, was found in a little chest floating upon the water. The people call themselves Chada, "The Beloved." In the city of Usumasa, on a site belonging to one of the oldest of the Chada families, is a well some fifteen hundred years old. Upon the stone curbing the word "Israel" is engraved.

Israelite Sea Voyages

More speculative is the proposition that ancient sea travelers from Israel and Phoenicia made their presence known to what would have then been the far-flung reaches of the world. The navies of Solomon and Hiram ranged far. Journeys were made to "Ophir" (I Kings 9:26-28). Many guesses have been made as to the location of this land which was the source of treasure. The theory that Ophir is Peru has little to be said for it. No etymological connection exists. But the fact remains

---

[44] Rodkinson, *Babylonian Talmud*, IV, Megilla, p. 49; Baba Kama, p. 180.

that the journeys sometimes were three years in duration (I Kings 10:22).

Evidence from Brazil of an early Phoenician voyage, long ignored as an elaborate and clever hoax, has found late respectability in the endorsement of Cyrus H. Gordon. Chiseled into a crude stone tablet in the language of the ancient Phoenicians is the inscription, "We are the Sons of Canaan from Sidon, the city of the king, commerce has cast us on this distant shore, a land of mountains." The tablet goes on to tell of ten Phoenician trading vessels that embarked from the ancient port of Ezion-Geber (near the modern Israeli town of Elath) on the Gulf of Aqaba, possibly in the seventh century B.C. Gordon has testified that "the alternatives are either that the inscription is genuine, or that the guy was a great prophet."[45]

Janet Greisch, writing in *Christianity Today*, notes the presence of a clan in east Tennessee with traditions of such ocean journeys. The people are known as Melungeons. They maintain a persistent tradition that their ancestors arrived on Phoenician ships centuries before Columbus. They are not Indian, Negroes, or Anglo-Saxons. Gordon says they are "Caucasians of Mediterranean descent.[46]

In October of 1970 *the Cincinnati Enquirer* carried an article about the re-examination of an inscription found in a burial mound in Tennessee in 1885. Cyrus Gordon said he discovered that "its five letters are in the writing style of Canaan, the 'promised land' of Israelites somewhere between the Jordan River and the Mediterranean." He translated the inscription to read "for the land of Judah." He concludes that the source of the inscription is an early migration of Jews, "probably to

45 "Archaeology, Before Columbus or the Vikings," *Time*, May 24, 1968, p. 62.

46 Janet Robler Griesch, "Jews First American Settlers," *Christianity Today*, November 6, 1970, p. 6.

escape the long hand of Rome after the disastrous Jewish defeats in AD 70 and 135."[47]

A recently excavated Maya Stela has been verified by Alexander von Wuthenau of the University of the Americas in Mexico City and by Cyrus Gordon as evidence that Mediterraneans lived in Mexico as long ago as A.D. 700. The Mexican stone is on display in the National Museum in Mexico City. It is a side view of a squat, scowling man wearing a large earring containing a Star of David.[48]

This new evidence in no way supports Mormon claims. The arrival of any Jews at the time assigned by Gordon is more than half a millennium too late to fit into the Mormon scheme of New World history. What it may indicate is that the energetic Jewish culture was available to fill spiritual and cultural vacuums *through-out* the pagan world from very early times.

Cognateness

Every country has its Jewish communities. Some are thoroughly integrated into the life of the nation. Some are ethnic and cultural islands. The survey of peoples identified as Lost Israel includes almost every nation. The evidence points to the energy inherent in the Jewish religio-culture. By now it is clear that the presence of that which seems to be Israelitish in origin does not necessarily point to racial or national descent from Abraham. To trace every hint of Jewishness back to the deportation of Samaria is absurd. This section calls attention to the fact it is not necessary to trace every hint of Jewishness to *any* Hebrew source at all.

The human race enjoys a certain cognateness; that is, proclivity toward certain kinds of religious and social

---

[47] Associated Press Dispatch, *Cincinnati Enquirer*, October 19, 1970.

[48] Associated Press Dispatch, *ibid.*, March 23, 1971.

expression that has no source other than the universal human spirit. The first chapter of Romans teaches that God holds mankind responsible for an innate awareness of His presence and basic nature because they are "clearly seen, being understood by the things that are made" (v. 20).

It follows, then, that isolated pagans may be aware of God even though they have never enjoyed contact with Hebrews and revealed religion. Religious awareness and forms of worship in particular instances may reflect nothing more than a racial connection with Adam. Particular forms of prayer, sacrifice, ceremony, and so forth, may seem to be Israelite or Hebrew, when in reality they are only human.

Cognateness opens the door to coincidence. Phenomena of language, religion, social custom, cultural patterns, personality traits, and the like may be merely combinations or arrangements of the mental and spiritual building blocks to which man is limited. These combinations may closely resemble others worked out elsewhere quite independently. Similarities may be coincidental. The principle is sound and ought not be ignored when considering possible sources of what appear to be traces of Hebrew culture. From Adam and from Noah mankind has potentially inherited religion as well as race. The religious heritage of man may surface in isolated circumstances but in similar expressions.

The Samarian deportation was only one avenue along which traveled Israelite culture into the world. Other deportations, vigorous proselyting, forced promiscuity, dispersion, and possible early Israelite sea voyages offer alternate explanations for the presence of what seems to be an almost universal Jewishness. The excellent record of the Jews of the Dispersion in maintaining their culture under adverse circumstances is testimony of the inherent vigor of that culture. The Jews have been a paradox. They have blended with every nation and been lost in none. Because Hebrew cultural patterns and religion have been almost universally available from the very earliest times, it is absurd to see in each appearance of Jewishness a necessary connection to the deportation of Samaria. Traditions of Israelite descent have traveled with the Jews. They have survived as a part of the total Jewish mind. They appear wherever the Hebrew culture has left a footprint. They are an indication of the tenacity of Jewishness. They do not establish the identity of a Lost Ten Tribes of Israel.

It is foolish for Armstrong to point to a white American and say, "You are of Israel's race because you are Anglo-Saxon." "Israel" never has been a race. In the melting pot of America, few can prove pure Anglo-Saxon heritage. To speak of a "chosen race" is an ethnological absurdity.

A Chinese-American who believes in God, who is circumcised as a normal medical practice, is named Dan, likes kosher pickles, and has Saturday off, is exhibiting "Jewish" cultural patterns. According to Armstrongite logic, these practices are indisputable proof that he is a descendant of one of the Lost Ten Tribes.

Israel Not Lost

An absolute essential of Armstrongism and British-Israelism is obviously a Lost Israel. By "lost" Armstrong does not mean merely politically defunct; he means nationally absent. The system requires more than just the lostness of the political entity called Israel; it requires the relocation of the people—all of them. Armstrong explains:

> History does record their captivity by Assyria, 721 through 718 B.C. They were removed from their cities, towns and farms in their northern part of Palestine, taken as slaves to Assyria, on the southern shores of the Caspian Sea.
> But by 604 to 585 B.C., when the southern kingdom of JUDAH was taken captive by Nebu-

51

chadnezzar of Babylon, the Assyrians had migrated northwest—and the Ten-Tribed Israelites with them!

Utterly Lost

They were utterly GONE!

They were lost from view!

How far northwest they proceeded, or where they finally settled, comes to a blank page in history.[49]

He also asserts: "The house of Israel did NOT return to Palestine with the Jews in the days of Ezra and Nehemiah, as some erroneously believe."[50]

The record of Scripture is II Kings 17:23-24. "Israel" in this text is understood by Armstrong to include men, women, and children. It is presupposed to include the rich and the poor, the old and the young, the master and the servant, the prince and the scavenger. When Israel was marched away, the real estate was denuded of humanity. Every town became a ghost town, every building a roost for owls, every farm the domain of the jackal. Armstrongism cannot have Israel in the British Isles unless they are out of the Ephraimite plain.

But the evidence, both Biblical and non-Biblical, is of the deportation of Israel in the sense of the removal of the aristocratic minority. The account in II Kings is far from exhaustive; it is almost totally lacking in details. When all the evidence pertinent to the question is sifted and reasonable and logical inferences are made, there emerges the conclusion that the deportation was of the political, military, industrial, and religious elite. Israel was deported in that the ruling class, that segment which made possible the political existence of the northern kingdom, was removed. The repeated romantic search for Lost Israel has been a child's game from the first. Israel has never been lost in that way.

---

49 *USBCP*, p. 152.
50 *Ibid.*, p. 89.

"Israel," even in national context, does not always mean the nation as a whole. In II Samuel 10:17 David gathered "all Israel" to cross the Jordan into the region where two and a half tribes are pictured as dwelling. As a matter of fact it was not a gathering of the total population, but of soldiers for a military campaign against the Syrians. Then the next year he sends "all Israel" into the same region (II Sam. 11:1), but he falls afoul of the charms of Bathsheba back in Jerusalem. Uriah, the wronged husband, refuses to cooperate with the lustful and devious David because the ark and Israel are encamped in the open (11:11). So "all Israel" is away on a military expedition while the "rest of the people" (II Sam. 12:28) are later gathered and taken to Rabbah to help Joab complete his campaign.

Similarly, Absalom and "all the elders of Israel" (II Sam. 17:4) are advised by Hushai to gather "all Israel" (v. 11) as though none of Israel were with David. And in verse 24 "all the men of Israel" are listed as the following of David.

"All the tribes of Israel" are interested in bringing David back (II Sam. 19:8-11, 41-43). In this case "all Israel" asserts that it has ten parts or votes in making any king; evidently it voted by "tribes." Then "every man of Israel" forsakes David for Sheba (20:1 f.), but Joab recruits an army "through all the tribes of Israel" in pursuit of him (20:14).

In II Samuel 24:2-9 the numbering of "all Israel" proves to be only a military census; but the account includes annexed districts that are in some other passages contrasted to Israel. In all these accounts, "Israel" is at most only the military class and seldom all of that.

While this study is brief and far from comprehensive, it is sufficient to demonstrate *the possibility* that the claims of Scripture that Israel was removed may be justified by the deportation of only an official-military aristocracy. If this is the case, then those heathen imports (II Kings 17:24) were to "possess" in the sense of being the ruling class in the subjugated countryside. The cities in the path of the invading army would have been ravaged and a tragic loss of life would have occurred, but a majority would have survived. As seen in the survey of II Samuel, "all Israel" is not always the majority.

The Concept of Shebet[51] ("Tribe")

The record of Scriptures is that when Israel was removed, none were left "but the *tribe* of Judah only" (II Kings 17:18). It is impossible to understand *shebet* here to mean absolutely no more or no less than the tribe of Judah. Much more than the tribe of Judah was included in the southern kingdom. For instance:

> "And when Rehoboam was come to Jerusalem, he assembled all the house of Judah, *with the tribe of Benjamin,* an hundred and fourscore thousand chosen men, which were warriors, to fight against the house of Israel, to bring the kingdom again to Rehoboam the son of Solomon" (I Kings 12:21).

As a parenthetical consideration, in this text "all the house of Judah" is the label given to the military force assembled. A survey of this kind of phraseology demonstrates that "all Judah" is also often used in a narrower sense than of the total nation.

It is clear that those constituting Judah were all those of *every* tribe who chose to gather under the standard (*shebet*) of Judah. Judah was the gathering of those who chose to be represented by the ruling class so

51 The word *shebet* has two basic meanings: (*a*) rod, staff, club, or sceptre; and (*b*) tribe. See Francis Brown, S. R. Driver, Charles Briggs, *A Hebrew and English Lexicon of the Old Testament* (Oxford: Clarendon Press, 1962), pp. 986-87.

identified. It is, therefore, reasonable to understand that Shalmaneser left no Israelite government; and, pending the establishment of a pro-Assyrian one, there was no *shebet* under which the people might rally except Judah. The word study shows that the primary meaning of the word in this connection is the sceptre or standard under which the general population might rally. Jeroboam won the ruling class (I Kings 11:31) which had earlier come to Samuel in Ramah (I Sam. 8:4) seeking a king, and these representatives assembled as clan heads at Mizpeh (I Sam. 10:21). In the section on evidence of a remaining population, it will be seen that precisely this kind of rallying under the headship of Judah took place.

If the viewpoint of the author of II Esdras reflected in some way the common idea of Lost Israel in the first century, perhaps the situation was one in which succeeding generations thought of the fate of such "shebatim" as being the fate of the nation or masses. This would not be without precedent.

The concept of *shebet* is an important consideration. It touches a very sensitive nerve in the Lost Tribes hunter. Armstrong is very explicit in explaining:

> "In 721-718 B.C. ISRAEL began to be carried away out of their land to Assyria (II Kings 17:23). They were soon *ALL* removed—completely. There was none left but the tribe of Judah only (II Kings 17:18). JUDAH, *only, remained.*"[52]

The Deportation of Judah

Because of the similarity of language used in Scripture for the respective deportations of Israel and Judah by Assyria and Babylonia, it is in order to determine the magnitude of the deportation of Jerusalem. The Book of Jeremiah closes with the observation that "thus Judah was carried away captive out of his own land" (52:27).

---

[52] *USBCP*, p. 89.

The affirmation is qualified or explained in the same chapter by the following inventory:

> This is the people whom Nebuchadrezzar carried away captive: in the seventh year three thousand Jews and three and twenty: In the eighteenth year of Nebuchadrezzar he carried away captive from Jerusalem eight hundred thirty and two persons: In the three and twentieth year of Nebuchadrezzar Nebuzaradan the captain of the guard carried away captive of the Jews seven hundred forty and five persons: all the persons were four thousand and six hundred (vv. 28-30).

This makes a total of 4,600 persons deported.

Although the total listed by the prophet is not a complete one for the whole series of deportations to Babylon, the context demonstrates a specialized narrow use of the tribal distinction "Judah," and that is the point being made here. The prisoner list given in II Kings 24 reinforces this point:

> And he carried away all Jerusalem, and all the princes, and all the mighty men of valour, even ten thousand captives, and all the craftsmen and smiths: none remained, save the poorest sort of the people of the land. And he carried away Jehoiachin to Babylon, and the king's mother, and the king's wives, and his officers, and the mighty of the land, those carried he into captivity from Jerusalem to Babylon. And all the men of might, even seven thousand, and craftsmen and smiths a thousand, all that were strong and apt for war, even them the king of Babylon brought captive to Babylon (vv. 14-16).

The above citations from Jeremiah and II Kings make it clear that Judah was "carried away captive" in that the ability of the nation to function was destroyed by the forced removal of the political, military, industrial, and socially elite. One does not have to be much of a student of ancient Near Eastern history to be aware that the "poorest sort of the people" were undoubtedly a large bloc of the population. Ten thousand or more princes, soldiers, craftsmen, and smiths were a minority as far as a head count would be concerned.

Even though "all Jerusalem" was deported in 597 B.C. (II Kings 24:14), Jerusalem continued to exist for eleven more years as the capital of a vassal kingdom ruled by the Babylonian appointee Zedekiah. Even the Babylonian account makes it clear that there was a nation left as far as population is concerned, and arrangements were made to establish a government after Jehoiakin and the national leaders had been removed:

> In the seventh year, in the month of Kislev, the Babylonian king mustered his troops, and, having marched to the land of Hatti, besieged the city of Judah, and on the second day of the month of Adar took the city and captured the king. *He appointed therein a king of his own choice*, received its heavy tribute and sent (them) to Babylon.[53] (Italics added.)

Eleven years after "all Jerusalem was taken captive" the city was again besieged by Nebuchadnezzar (II Kings 25:1-2). It took the Babylonians eighteen months to penetrate the walls of the city and take possession of it. Another massive deportation took place and again the poor were left to be vinedressers and husbandmen (II Kings 25:11-12). Nebuchadnezzar appointed the pro-Babylonian Gedaliah as governor of the land (II Kings 25:22). The Jews who had fled to Moab and Edom and those in exile among the Ammonites and other neighboring areas heard that the king of Babylon had left a remnant (not necessarily a minority) of Judah and there rejoined them (Jer. 40:11-12). Yet, Jeremiah had predicted:

> The cities of the south shall be shut up, and

[53] Thomas, *op. cit.*, p. 80.

none shall open them: Judah shall be carried
away captive all of it, it shall be wholly carried
away captive (13:19).

This form of hyperbole was not confined to Scripture. The record of Tiglath-pileser III reflects it in the
record he left of the downfall of Pekah:

Israel (lit. "Omri-Land" *Bit Humria*) ... all
its inhabitants (and) their possessions I led to
Assyria. They overthrew their king Pekah (*Pa-ca-
ha*) and I placed Hoshea (A-*u si*) as king over
them.[54]

Despite the claim that Israel and all its inhabitants were
deported, the fact is that after Hoshea succeeded Pekah
(II Kings 15:27-31), he ruled in Samaria for nine years,
up to the conquest by Shalmaneser.

Similarity in language also is seen in the record that
the Lord removed Israel and Judah "out of his sight" (II
Kings 17:18; 23:27) and cast them "from his presence"
(II Kings 24:20; Jer. 52:3). *If Judah did not suffer a
complete national removal, then the same qualification
may be placed on the language when it is used in
reference to Israel when describing the same kind of
thing.* Again, the judgmental relocation of a representative group called Judah or Israel would justify the sweep-
ing hyperbole here and in those places where it appears
in other prophetic sections. Another example is found in
Lamentations 1:3, where Jeremiah, himself sitting in the
ashes of the holy city, says that "Judah is gone into
captivity." Such figures are used to indicate the disfavor
of the Lord, without always involving the physical or
geographical location of the one so cursed. God speaking
through Moses declared that a priest who defiled himself
with unholy things would be "cut off from my presence:
I am the LORD" (Lev. 22:3). David in his great psalm of

54 J. B. Pritchard (ed.), *Ancient Near Eastern Texts
Relating to the Old Testament* (Princeton: Princeton
University Press, 1955), p. 284.

repentance prayed to God, "Cast me not away from thy presence" (51:11).

There is, of course, no questioning a devastating displacement of people from Israel. But the point is that the language used is often figurative to the extent that it is reasonable and Scriptural to understand it to mean less than a complete deportation of the nation. The judgment of God was complete, although the deportation was not necessarily complete in the sense of leaving no one behind. Figurative language is in obvious use here. The lamentations are that Israel and Judah were taken "out of his sight" and "from his presence." God can see Assyria from where He "sits" and Babylonia is not beyond His omnipresence.

Geographical Extent of the Deportation

Armstrong visualizes the systematic scouring of the land and the denuding of it of people. The account is, "Then the king of Assyria came up throughout all the land, and went up to Samaria, and besieged it three years" (II Kings 17:5). The deportation was from Samaria "and the cities thereof" and here the imported heathen rulers were brought. But the Assyrian army was not large enough to diffuse itself over the entire land, nor is there any record of an interest in doing so. Wars do not decimate general populations, even in areas where battles are fought, as is popularly thought. Even the history of modern warfare with its devilishly sophisticated and efficient weaponry demonstrates the fact that devastation and death are localized. The general population avoids direct contact with military action. In the terrible destruction of Jerusalem in A.D. 70, Jesus indicated that there would be safety in flight (Matt. 24:16; Luke 21:21).

As an example, few cities have been more systematically razed by invading armies than Berlin in the closing days of World War II. An excerpt from a history of the Battle of Berlin goes:

Zhukov's forces now hammered their way into the city, leaving a vast sea of rubble in their wake. Russian troops took Tempelhof airfield on April 26 and advanced methodically into the heart of the city—Unter den Linden and the Tiergarten. Some German units fought frantically street-by-street and building-by-building. But their defenses proved futile and only added to the fiery destruction of the city.[55]

By the spring of 1945, the city was little more than rubble, having been heavily and repeatedly bombed by the Allies and severely damaged by artillery fire. The Soviet forces then raped, pillaged, and slaughtered the defenseless civilian population. Yet, in all this the population of the city in 1945 was 2,932,432, well over half of the 1939 count of 4,332,242.

Wars do not dramatically influence general populations or population growth rates in a nation, even in the years of actual conflict. To credit the Assyrian army with the successful and complete scraping of a nation the size of Israel is to overestimate it, even in the light of Assyrian battle records. The Bible does not tell of an Assyrian expeditionary force large enough for such a task.

To borrow a summation on this point from Allen Godbey in his work *The Lost Tribes a Myth:*

> We can get from this chapter in Kings nothing more than the deportation of the controlling aristocrats. The expression "ten tribes" is not used, and only the Ephraimite plain is involved, as the limits of the subsequent "Samaritan" country steadily remind us.[56]

The Assyrian Record of the Deportation

Assyrian inscriptions record the fall of Samaria in

55 David Eggenberger, *A Dictionary of Battles* (New York: Thomas Y. Crowell Co., 1967), p. 52.

56 Godbey, *op. cit.,* p. 11.

particular and the imperial policy pursued by Assyria during that period in general. The years 1100-745 B.C. saw the relapse and then the recovery of Assyrian power. Samaria fell as a part of the Assyrian plan for reclamation and expansion.

The Policy of Tiglath-pileser III (*ca.* 745 B.C.)

The expansion of Assyria under Ashur-nasir-pal II to the west included an unopposed march to the Mediterranean, the work of Shalmaneser III, struggles with the Urartu and Bit-adini, and other campaigns in that direction.

Shalmaneser IV was forced into further campaigns against Urartu, the last of which in 774 B.C. was as unsuccessful as the rest had been. Defeats in the north led to fresh trouble in the west. The close of his reign saw Assyria in a weakened state.

Enter Tiglath-pileser III (745-727 B.C., identified as Pul in II Kings 15:19-20). This Assyrian emperor-general took his seat on the vacant throne in 745 B.C., and "was to restore, and more than restore to the Assyrians, the dominions held by Shalmaneser III and Adad-nirari III."[57]

A century prior to the reign of Tiglath-pileser III Assyrian policy came to be more than one of raiding, sacking, exacting tribute, and retreating. Of this expanded vision, Sidney Smith observes:

> The course of the almost yearly campaigns can be traced for over sixty years, and their importance is great; for in them is to be found the proof of a definite intention to establish *permanent rule* over the southern marches of Assyria and the western lands as far as the Mediterranean and to exercise suzerainty over the kingdoms adjacent to the new borders; in other words, *the establishment of an Assyrian empire*

[57] "The Foundation of the Assyrian Empire," *Cambridge Ancient History* (New York: Macmillan, 1925), III, 32.

became the aim of royal policy. This policy was
faithfully executed by a succession of monarchs,
not always with immediate success, but with a
persistence remarkable in the history of western
Asia.[58] (Italics added.)

Tiglath-pileser III injected new life into the faltering
program of empire building. The pivotal question is this:
*Did the practice of national deportation augment this
policy?* It would not be necessary to relocate a nation in
its entirety to make possible a system of permanent rule.
It seems reasonable to assume that if the replacing of the
ruling class with a military dictatorship would have
served the avowed purpose of the western campaigns,
then the Assyrians would have settled for that. Total
deportation would not have necessarily solved the problem of recurring nationalistic rebellion; it might have
simply relocated it. Such nationalism would have been
destroyed only by deporting a nation in a way that
would accomplish the dissolution of the nation. (It is
interesting that Armstrong, who insists upon a total
deportation, is the very one who heatedly denies that
the nation was dissolved.)

What the Assyrian monarchs were interested in was
ruling subjugated peoples in such a way as to gain from
their tribute, not in using them to play a game of
national musical chairs. Also, it would seem unlikely
that the Assyrians would have unnecessarily interrupted
for a year or two the ability of a conquered nation to
produce revenue. Total deportation did not fit the policy of Tiglath-pileser. Commenting on his, Sidney Smith
notes:

> In later times there is evidence that in cer-
> tain districts Assyrian policy was satisfied to
> keep a native Assyrian party in power, and we
> know that in Bit-Zamani in the north Ammeba'-
> ali lost his life in the Assyrian cause. . . .

58 *Ibid.*, p. 9.

Modern writers have expressed varying views on the system of wholesale deportation as practiced by this monarch. While some have considered that it was the only means by which the Assyrians could govern lands to which they were entitled by force alone, others have seen the seed of future weakness in the disruption of the ties of patriotism and religion. However this may be, it should be noted that this sudden transference of population would not appear so strange in the ancient east, where tribes would of their own free-will leave their lands to seek fresh homes, and also that Tiglath-pileser, who merely extended the practice of his predecessors, was guided by a political object of some importance for the administration of new territories.[59]

To speak of wholesale and massive deportation is not to imply complete or even majority deportation. The purpose was to establish a rule that could be maintained without the expense of repeated, constant military intimidation. The purpose was not to dissolve or relocate for the sake of devastation itself.

The Testimony of Assyrian Inscriptions

In the years 742-740 B.C., Tiglath-pileser conducted a three-year siege of the city of Arpad. During the time he was so occupied, the absence of the Assyrian army was seized upon as an occasion for the formation of some kind of confederacy to oppose him; and the leader of the confederacy was a certain Azriau of Yaudi.[60] This Azriau has been disputedly identified as Azariah or Uzziah, king of Judah (II Kings 15:27). The annalistic record found in Calah is an account of the military expedition against the disobedient nations, a list of the

[59] *Ibid.*, pp. 15, 41.

[60] Thomas, *op. cit.*, pp. 54-56. The text is on a broken and mutilated stone slab giving part of the royal annals and inscribed clay tablets originally set up in the temple of Nabu (Nebo) at Nimrud.

areas conquered, a list of the tribute paid to Tiglath-
pileser III by the vanquished, and the following record
of the shuffling of the population:

> An officer of mine I installed as governor
> over them. (I deported) 30,300 inhabitants from
> their cities and settled them in the province of
> the town Ku [...] 1,223 inhabitants I settled
> in the province of the Allaba country.[61]

It is in keeping with Assyrian policy that not all nor even
a majority of the inhabitants were deported: only
30,000 from all the cities conquered. An officer is left as
governor over the remaining citizenry.

This is the place to observe that the statistics given
in the annalistic records are undoubtedly optimistic.
Even a cursory reading of the texts left by Near Eastern
monarchs assures one that modesty was not the prevailing attitude. Little if any notice is ever given of the
military reverses that certainly took place. Only the
most glowing terms[62] are used for themselves. It is a
consensus among scholars that the numbers given are
often exaggerations. Most of the tallies are in round
numbers, and it would certainly be out of harmony with
the spirit of the language for the estimates to be pessi-
mistic. Those kings seem to have given themselves the
benefit of any doubt.

About the year 738 B.C. Damascus (although Syria
was under the nominal control of Tiglath-pileser) and
Samaria acted together as allies. Tiglath-pileser feared
the growing power of Rezon of Damascus. Philistia was
the object of an Assyrian campaign in 734. This was for
the purpose of ensuring "a position in that southern land
which would make it impossible for Rezon to look in

61 Pritchard, *op. cit.*, p. 283.

62 E.g., the Taylor Prism relating Sennacherib's siege
of Jerusalem: "As for Hezekiah, the awful splendor of
my lordship overwhelmed him. . . ." See Thomas, *op.
cit.*, pp. 64 ff.

that direction for aid."[63] The presence of an Assyrian army in Philistia rearranged the politics of Israel and Judah. Israel and Damascus had formed an alliance against Judah with the result that young Ahaz of Judah turned to the Assyrian king for an alliance. The aid was given. In 733 Samaria and Damascus were reduced. II Kings 15 tells of Pekah's flight from Samaria and the destruction of various strong points in Israel.

Assyrian stone slabs giving part of the royal annals and inscribed clay tablets record that Tiglath-pileser deported from the cities of Rezon certain numbers of the people. Relocated were 800 from one city, 750 and 550 respectively from the "16 districts of the country of Damascus."[64]

In the previously cited record, an account is left of his defeat of Pekah in which he claims to have deported "all its inhabitants," *yet Hoshea ruled in Samaria for the following nine years.*

In the seventh year of Hoshea, Samaria was besieged by Shalmaneser V. Three years later it was captured by an Assyrian king (II Kings 17:5-6; 18:9-10) whose name is not mentioned. Josephus says it was Shalmaneser.[65] Two years later Samaria made an alliance with Hamath, Arpad, and Damascus in an effort to overthrow Assyrian rule. The revolt failed. The deported Israelites from the city were replaced by heathen from the countries listed in II Kings.

Whether a deportation of the inhabitants and the settlement of captives of various nationalities, including Arabs in Samaria, took place in 722-21 B.C. or subsequently is not definitely known. This procedure, the preliminary to the establishment of Samaria as an Assyrian province, may not have been enforced until after

63 Smith, *op. cit.*, p. 38.
64 Pritchard, *loc. cit.*
65 *Antiq.* IX. xiv. 1.

the remnant of Israel joined in the remarkable coalition directed against Sargon in 720 B.C.

The policy of replacing the political-military administration with loyal Assyrians is seen in the record by Sargon II (721-705 B.C.):

> I smash [ed] like a flood-storm the country of Hamath (*A-ma-at-tu*) in its entire [extent.] I br[ought its] ki[ng] Iaubi'di as well as his family (and) his warriors in fett[ers], as the prisoner (contingent) of his country, to Assyria. From these (prisoners) I set [up a troop] of 300 chariots (and) 600 mounted men. . . .
>
> I se[ttled] 6,300 Assyrians of reliable [disposition] in the country of Hamath and installed an officer of mine as go[vernor] over them, imposing upon th[em] (the payment) of tri[bute].[66]

Of Samaria he claims:

> I besieged and conquered Samaria (*Sa-me-ri-na*), led away as booty 27,290 inhabitants of it. I formed from among them a contingent of 50 chariots and made remaining (inhabitants) assume their (social) positions. I installed over them an officer of mine and imposed upon them the tribute of the former king (*Display Inscription*).[67]
>
> At the beginning [of my rule . . . the city of the Sa]marians I [besieged and conquered . . .] who let me achieve my victory . . . carried off prisoner [27,290 of the people who dwelt in it; from among them I equipped 50 chariots for my royal army units . . . the city of Samaria] I restored and made it more habitable than before. [I brought into it] people of the countries conquered by my own hands. [My official I set over them as district-governor and] imposed upon them tribute as on an Assyrian (city). . . . I made to mix with each other; the market price . . . (*Annals*, 10-18).[68]

---

66 Pritchard, *op. cit.*, p. 284.
67 Thomas, *op. cit.*, p. 60.
68 *Ibid.*, p. 59.

> [The governor of Sa]maria who had consort-
> ed with he king who opposed me not to do
> service and not to bring tribute . . . and they did
> battle. I clashed with them in the power of the
> great gods, my lords, and counted as spoil 27,280
> people together with their chariots. . . (Nimrud
> Prism, iv. 25-41).[69]

The picture in the Assyrian record is precisely that
of the removal of a significant number of people,
27,290, of the ruling and military class, and the imposi-
tion of a pro-Assyrian hierarchy upon the remaining
masses.

Evidence of a Remaining Israelite Population

If "Israel" were banished to the land of the Two
Rivers only in the sense that that segment of the population was deported which gave the nation political cohe-
siveness, then it is to be expected that an indication
would be available of the continued presence of subjugated Israelite masses in the northern area.

If the chronicler of Scripture intended to say that
the land of Israel was denuded of Israelite population,
then there should be no further reference to their presence after the fall of Samaria. Quite the opposite is true.

Israel attends the passover of Hezekiah. In his deter-
mination to have a religious revival, Hezekiah sent invitations to all the people of the Lord to attend a passover.
This took place some years after the fall of Samaria; and
the king seems to be unaware that the ten tribes are lost
or removed in a body, for the invitation includes all
Israel. Armstrong and company should note that Ephraim and Manasseh are mentioned in particular:

> And Hezekiah sent to all Israel and Judah,
> and wrote letters also to Ephraim and Manasseh,
> that they should come to the house of the LORD
> at Jerusalem, to keep the passover unto the
> LORD God of Israel (II Chron. 30:1).

[69] *Ibid.,* p. 60.

The messengers bearing the invitations were instructed to cover all the area of original Israel—Dan to Beer-Sheba—and to invite Israel and Judah (II Chron. 30:5-6).

> So the posts passed from city to city through the country of Ephraim and Manasseh even unto Zebulun: but they laughed them to scorn, and mocked them. Nevertheless divers of Asher and Manasseh and of Zebulun humbled themselves, and came to Jerusalem (II Chron. 30:10-11).

> For a multitude of the people, even many of Ephraim, and Manasseh, Issachar, and Zebulun, had not cleansed themselves, yet did they eat the Passover otherwise than it was written. But Hezekiah prayed for them, saying, The good LORD pardon every one... II Chron. 30:18).

> And all the congregation of Judah, with the priests and the Levites, and all the congregation that came out of Israel, and the strangers that came out of the land of Israel, and that dwelt in Judah, rejoiced (II Chron. 30:25).

In this last citation the distinction is made between the "congregation" that came out of Israel and the "strangers" (proselytes from among the transplanted heathen) that came from the northern territory.

Israel attends the Passover of Josiah. In the year 628 B.C., three years before Nabopolassar, father of Nebuchadnezzar, founded the independent monarchy of Babylon, so soon to be the antagonist of Judah, the work of reformation had been started by Josiah. The vigorous campaign was not restricted to Judah, for Josiah had taken advantage of the weakened and battered Assyrians and virtually resumed possession of the northern plain. The record of Scripture affirms that Israel was represented at this passover as they had been at the one called by Hezekiah:

68

> And the children of Israel that were present
> kept the passover at that time, and the feast of
> unleavened bread seven days. And there was no
> passover like to that kept in Israel from the days
> of Samuel the prophet; neither did all the kings
> of Israel keep such a passover as Josiah kept, and
> the priests, and the Levites, and all Judah and
> Israel that were present, and the inhabitants of
> Jerusalem (II Chron. 35:17-18).

Among those contributing money for the repair of
the Temple by Josiah are those of "Manasseh and Ephraim, and of all the remnant of Israel" (II Chron. 34:9).

It is not strange to see people of the northern
kingdom respond to the invitations of Hezekiah and
Josiah. From the occasion of the defection of Jeroboam,
large numbers of them chose to be identified with the
"shebet" of Judah. When God instructed Rehoboam not
to make war with Jeroboam, the commandment was
given not only to Judah and Benjamin, but also to "the
remnant of the people" (I Kings 12:23).

A multitude returned under Asa. It was not just at
the occasion of the defection of Jeroboam that the
masses of Israel were called upon to choose between the
northern and southern thrones as rallying points. The
record is that there was a constant gathering of northern
Israel into southern Judah after the dramatic breakup of
the nation. Again Ephraim and Manasseh receive special
mention:

> And he gathered all Judah and Benjamin,
> and the strangers with them out of Ephraim and
> Manasseh, and out of Simeon: for they fell to
> him out of Israel *in abundance* (II Chron. 15:9).

Kings of Judah are called "King of Israel." The fact
that Jehoshaphat, fourth king of the southern monarchy, is called the "king of Israel" (II Chron. 21:1-2),
whereas Ahab, Ahaziah, and Joram were the successive
kings to occupy the throne in Samaria, is significant.

Ahaz, contemporary with Pekah and Hoshea, is given the same title (II Chron. 28:19). Advocates of the theory of the Lost Ten Tribes of Israel insist fervently that the terms "Israel" and "Judah" are mutually exclusive when used in a national sense. The promises, therefore, made to Israel can never be fulfilled in peoples labeled Jew or Judah. But both Old and New Testaments use the terms interchangeably, except where the distinction is being made between the northern and southern monarchies during their political existence. And not too much care is given even in this case. The claim cannot be strictly defended that the appellation Israel was not applied to Judah till after the destruction of Samaria.

If the deportation of Israel was a complete denuding of the land of its people, and the only occupants in the succeeding years were heathen imports, then there is not a sound argument for the accuracy of the Scriptural record which affirms that the people of the ten-tribed nation were still being dealt with by kings of the surviving southern kingdom for more than a hundred years. The testimony points to a continued merging of the peoples into one nation in Judah, to the exclusion of those who chose to be mingled with the non-Israelite "strangers." Thus, in later times, the fortunes of Israel were such as were enjoyed or endured only as a part of Judah.

"Israel" returns from Babylon. The "house of Israel" was in captivity in Babylon with Judah (Ezek. 3:1-15). The territorial empire of Babylon was coextensive with that of the earlier Assyrian empire. That part of "Israel" having spent more than a century in the Mesopotamian region is now to be dealt with. The resident prophet, in his vision of the valley of dry bones, was made to understand that the "house of Israel" would be returned "into the land of Israel" (Ezek. 37:11-12). Jeremiah had promised that the house of Israel would return from the north country to dwell again in their land (23:8). Cyrus the Great, king of

Persia, had made a proclamation in Babylon to all of the Jews "throughout all his kingdom" that:

> The LORD God of heaven hath given me all the kingdoms of the earth; and he hath charged me to build him an house at Jerusalem, which is in Judah. Who is there among you of all his people? his God be with him, and let him go up to Jerusalem, which is in Judah, and build the house of the LORD God of Israel, (he is the God,) which is in Jerusalem (Ezra 1:2-3).

If the ten tribes were not included in this proclamation, then they were not of "all his people"—not the people of God.

When the Temple was dedicated, those doing it were not two-tribed Judah, but twelve-tribed Israel:

> And the children of Israel, the priests, and the Levites, and the rest of the children of the captivity, kept the dedication of this house of God with joy, And offered at the dedication of this house of God an hundred bullocks, two hundred rams, four hundred lambs; and for a sin offering for all Israel, twelve he goats, according to the number of the tribes of Israel (Ezra 6:16-17).

In the Book of Ezra the people of God are called Jews eight times and Israel forty times. In Nehemiah they are called Jews eleven times and Israel twenty-two times.

If only Judah returned from Babylon and the house of Israel remained lost, to be found centuries later in the British Isles or elsewhere, then how are the children of Ephraim and Manasseh found in Jerusalem after the return from Babylonian captivity? This is recorded in I Chronicles:

> So all Israel were reckoned by genealogies; and, behold, they were written in the book of the kings of Israel and Judah, who were carried away to Babylon for their transgression. Now the

71

first inhabitants that dwelt in their possessions in
their cities were, the Israelites, the priests, Levites, and the Nethinims. And in Jerusalem dwelt
of the children of Judah, and of the children of
Benjamin, and of the children of Ephraim, and
Manasseh (9:1-3).

These genealogies were public records kept from the
beginning of the Hebrew nation of every individual, as
well as the family tribe to which he belonged. "The
book of the kings of Israel" does not refer to the two
canonical books of Scripture, but to authenticated
copies of those registers. They were carried with the
great number of Israelites that took refuge in Judah at
the invasion of Shalmaneser. Apparently they were kept
during the Babylonian captivity (I Chron. 3:17-24). The
statement above refers to the first returned exiles. Almost all the names appear in Nehemiah 11. Ephraim and
Manasseh are again named. At a time when Armstrong
teaches they are on their way to becoming the United
States and Great Britain, the Bible places them in Jerusalem claiming tribal possessions.

The "lost sheep of the house of Israel." Although it
is true that the appellation Jew is used 174 times in the
New Testament, it is difficult to conceive of the first-
century Jews as being under the impression that Israel
was a lost people and a dead issue. That name appears
75 times. The claim by Armstrong that the house of
Israel was in the British Isles notwithstanding, Jesus
identified the house of Israel with the Jewish inhabitants
of Palestine.

The attempt is made by the British-Israel segment of
Lost Tribes hunters to picture as peoples of separate and
distinct histories the Jews and the "dispersed among the
Gentiles." This dichotomy is imposed upon the language
of the Pharisees when they spoke concerning an enig-
matic promise made by the Master:

Ye shall seek me, and shall not find me: and
where I am, thither ye cannot come. Then said

the Jews among themselves, Whither will he go, that we shall not find him? will he go unto the dispersed among the Gentiles, and teach the Gentiles? (John 7:34-35).

J. H. Allen comments on this:

> This very question reveals the fact that the Jews knew that the ten tribes were dispersed among the nations, and that they could not go to them. They also comprehended the fact that, if this man called Christ should prove to be the long-expected Messiah, he did know where the lost people were, and could go to them. It is also an admission from the chief men of Judah, that a portion of the race were [sic] lost.[70]

But the record remains that Jesus commissioned the twelve:

> ... saying, Go not into the way of the Gentiles, and into any city of the Samaritans enter ye not. But go rather to the lost sheep of the house of Israel (Matt. 10:5-6).

This was not some kind of prophetic commission to be obeyed after the resurrection and subsequent spreading of the gospel and the church. This descriptive label, borrowed from Jeremiah (50:17), was applied to the inhabitants of Judaea. The Synoptics are clear that the ministry of Jesus and the Twelve, before the crucifixion, was confined to Galilee, Judaea, and Perea, and a brief exceptional foray into Samaria. The argument here is clinched by the scene on the borders of Tyre and Sidon as Jesus speaks to a Gentile woman. He is asked by the woman of Canaan to heal her daughter. When He does so, He makes it clear that the case is an exception to His stated policy:

> ... I am not sent but unto the lost sheep of the house of Israel. Then came she and wor-

[70] Allen, *op. cit.*, p. 135.

shipped him, saying, Lord, help me. But he answered and said, It is not meet to take the children's bread, and to cast it to dogs (Matt. 15:24-26).

If the "lost sheep of the house of Israel" had been established for centuries in Great Britain, or elsewhere, or if this ministry could only be carried out in some millennial period yet future, then Jesus failed. If Israel were in the isles of North Atlantic, then the very localized ministry of Jesus missed them altogether. And if Judah or the Jews are not also to be identified as the "lost sheep of the house of Israel," then Jesus spent His ministry among the wrong people.

Anna the prophetess. Strong evidence of a remaining Israelite population is found in the fact that Anna the prophetess (Luke 2:36) could trace her ancestry back to Asher. The real estate allotment of the eighth son of Jacob was the district that ran north from Carmel along the sea shore (Josh. 19:24-31). If the Samarian deportation was of the tribes *in toto*, then it would have been impossible for the genealogy of Anna to have survived.

The "dispersed." The argument that Israel and Judah were divided after the death of Solomon, never to enjoy joint destinies again, is strange in the light of the fact that the Jews of the dispersion are regarded as including all twelve tribes (Acts 26:7; James 1:1). The salutation in James is addressed to those among all the tribes who have become Christians and whose dispersion was further prompted by the persecution directed at the church. The reference to the twelve tribes in Acts speaks of all Jewry.

Evidence from Archaeology

At this writing the excavation of the cities in the northern area of Palestine has included work at Shechem, Tirzah (Tell el-Farak), Samaria, Megiddo, and

Hazor. Key sites are Samaria and Shechem. The systematic excavation of the cities of Israel is in its primary stage. Of these, Shechem enjoys the most complete documentation.

The evidence at Shechem. G. Ernest Wright points out that the reoccupation of Shechem after the retaliation of Shalmaneser against the conspiracy of Hoshea is represented by Stratum six. He notes that:

> The presence of foreigners in the country is attested by a considerable quantity of "Assyrian Palace Ware," a pottery which followed Mesopotamian models, though most of it was locally made. Yet little of Stratum VI remains.[71]

But the critical conclusion of the examination of the pottery of Stratum six is

> The fact that most of the pottery follows earlier Palestinian tradition, except for the bowls made on Mesopotamian models, *indicates that not all the people of the reoccupation were foreigners by any means.* In any event, foreigners and natives quickly adapted to the situation.[72] (Italics added.)

The evidence at Samaria. Parallel interpretation is given to the artifacts from the site of ancient Samaria. The report is:

> As negative evidence, it may be noted that a considerable number of late seventh century forms occur in Period VIII, but are not found in VII. Also a good deal of the Period VI wares is found in the same deposits as the new ones of VII, and would appear to have continued side by side with it.
> . . . It is entirely probable that the capture of

[71] G. Ernest Wright, *Shechem, the Biography of a Biblical City* (New York: McGraw-Hill Book Co., 1965), p. 164.

[72] *Ibid.,* p. 166.

Samaria by the Assyrians and the *partial deportation* of the inhabitants replaced by new settlers from elsewhere, would introduce a number of new forms of pottery, which would be found together with wares resembling those of the earlier period.[73] (Italics added.)

The lion plague. The episode of the lion plague is viewed by proponents of Lost Tribes theories as clear evidence that the land was made completely desolate of people. The record is:

> And so it was at the beginning of their dwelling there, that they feared not the LORD: therefore the LORD sent lions among them, which slew some of them. Wherefore they spake to the king of Assyria, saying, The nations which thou hast removed, and placed in the cities of Samaria, know not the manner of the God of the land: therefore he hath sent lions among them, and, behold, they slay them, because they know not the manner of the God of the land. Then the king of Assyria commanded, saying, Carry thither one of the priests whom ye brought from thence; and let them go and dwell there, and let him teach them the manner of the God of the land (II Kings 17:25-27).

The account is seized upon by Armstrong thus:

> It is these foreigners who were living in the land of Samaria in the time of Christ, and who were called Samaritans in the Gospel records. It is well to keep that in mind. For the Samaritans of the New Testament were not in any sense a racial mixture with the Israelites. Only *one* individual—a priest—returned from among the captive Israelites to teach the newly planted Gentiles the corrupted religion of Israel (II Kings 17:27-28).[74]

73 J. W. Crowfoot, G. M. Crowfoot, and Kathleen Kenyon, "Israelite Pottery," *The Objects from Samaria* (London: Palestine Exploration Fund, 1957), p. 98.

74 *USBCP*, pp. 87, 88.

The absence of true religion during this period does not prove the absence of an Israelite people. The apostasy of the nation for many generations has become proverbial. The Israelites had become as pagan as the imported rulers. The removal of the leaders of the people and any righteous and faithful that might have been among them would have contributed to still further degeneration of the spiritual life of those left behind.

The incursion of lions was an act of God. Perhaps God used the natural circumstance of the change in administration in this judgment. There is some indication that one of the principal tasks of ancient Near Eastern monarchs was to keep control of the lion population. A change in the ruling class and the period of transition may have been the occasion of this reminder from heaven of the disfavor of God.

The text is clear that this plague was directed at the imported aliens and their paganism and superstition, but does not claim that Israel was completely absent.

Logistics of Deportation

To say that the Assyrian expedition relocated a nation reasonably intact the size of Israel, may be a substitution of words for logic and reason. This is not to categorically deny the possibility. But the question of logistics is a reasonable one and important enough in this context to demand at least a glance.

The account in Scripture is that the exiles were taken from Samaria and its cities. The exiles were resettled in the Assyrian cities of Halah, Habor by the river Gozan, and in the cities of the Medes (II Kings 17:6; 18:11; II Chron. 5:26). The distance to be walked by these people (of all ages) was 300-600 miles. Making an extremely conservative estimate of the population of the northern kingdom at one million, it is apparent that the question of logistics must be asked. To move a million or even half a million people that many miles, provide the necessities of life for them, and preserve them for the foreign occupation of territories is quite a feat. Witness the Exodus. It is a situation calling for experts to move that number of well-conditioned, regimented military personnel.

A study of the Nazi efforts in deportation in the late 1930s gives insight into the problems involved in massive relocations of civilian population. Even with a railroad system available and with the fiendish efficiency of the SS, it was found that moving large numbers of civilians was an expensive and difficult task. For example:

> In December 1939, the Commander in Chief of the East, Field Marshal Blaskowitz, reported that the children arrived in the deportation trains frozen to death and that people were dying of hunger in the reception villages. The death rate among Jewish deportees to Lublin province was 30 per cent.[75]

The Nazis and the Assyrians were equally infamous in their respective heydays for the unbelievable inhumanity with which they treated their enemies. To envision the Assyrian army making the necessary arrangements to move such a number of men, women, and children such a distance in such a way as to accomplish the arrival of a reasonably intact nation is to be in danger of naiveté. Of course if no attempt was made to ensure their safety or even their survival, then the situation would be genocide and not deportation.

And then the matter of an equally massive immigration must be considered, for the human traffic was also moving east to west. The logistics aspect of the problem seems to be overwhelming when the reverse relocation of Assyrians to the cities of Samaria is to be explained (II Kings 17:24).

[75] Nora Levin, *The Holocaust, The Destruction of European Jewry 1933-1945* (New York: Thomas Y. Crowell Co., 1968), p. 181.

Also the cities to which Israelites were taken were not the same ones from which replacements came (II Kings 17:6, 24; I Chron. 5:26). If a million or so people vacated these areas, was the population decimated? Were these cities left to the jackals and owls? Were those cities populous enough to withstand such a population drain?

From the viewpoint of logistics, it is easier to envision the population shifts of II Kings 17 as that of large segments of the aristocracy than to imagine the entire population on the move.

Summary and Conclusions

The Biblical record, carefully studied, and the Assyrian record agree that the Samarian deportation was of the military, political, and industrial aristocracy. "Israel" as the national administration was deported and replaced by a leadership loyal to Assyria. The evidence from the Bible is of a remaining and continuing Israelite population. The testimony of the archaeologists is in agreement. The Jewish nation at the beginning of the intertestamental period was a twelve-tribed nation. The localized ministry of Jesus was to the "lost sheep of the house of Israel." The unreliable testimony from apocryphal literature is an insufficient argument to the contrary.

It is Scripturally and historically unjustified to speak of Israel as being lost in the sense of being nationally intact but unidentified. Scripture and history show that the northern kingdom did not suffer the kind of lostness that will permit Armstrongism to be true.

3 "IT'S IN YOUR BIBLE"

Armstrongism makes a great show of being Bible based. A monotonous theme of broadcast, publication, and lecture is that Armstrongite "truth" is obvious from even the most cursory reading of the Bible. But the claim that "it's in your Bible" is, of itself, insufficient ground for the kind of confidence Armstrong inspires in his many followers.

There are many systems of eisegesis—that is, reading *into* Scripture the particulars of a religious system which is, in turn, predicated upon extra-Scriptural presuppositions. Armstrongism is one of them. Anyone can wave the Bible about and claim it as the source of his doctrine. Scripture has been lifted from context and has "proved" everything from Rosicrucianism to snake-handling. Even Satan quotes Scripture (Matt. 4:6).

Armstrong announces that the rejoicing can begin because the "key" has been found and truth is once again available. This claim is suspect on the face of it. Scripture is not locked. It never has been. God is not a mischievous sovereign who has given a revelation for which He will hold man responsible, but who has been playing "hide the thimble" with the key that enables man to understand that revelation. We do not ascribe infallibility to the great Bible scholars of the ages. But the Augustines, Luthers, Calvins, and myriad learners who have followed in their train cannot be dismissed with nothing more than a wave of the hand. Moreover, anyone who allows Armstrong to stampede him into flippantly passing over two millennia of Bible scholarship so that he can "expect startling, amazing, eye-opening *facts* until now hidden from your eyes"[1] is not looking for serious truth but for a sideshow.

It is characteristic of cultism to claim the key to revealed truth. Armstrong is just one of the crowd. The Christian Science sect was born with Mary Baker Eddy's *Science and Health with a Key to the Scriptures.* Ellen G. White interprets the Word for Seventh-day Adventists. The *Book of Mormon* is the sieve through which Mormons strain Scripture. Charles Taze Russell and his successor Judge J. F. Rutherford are the doctrinarians for the Jehovah's Witnesses cult. Roman Catholicism claims that the priest must interpret Scripture for the laity. God has not entrusted Armstrong with the key to truth any more than He has any of the others.

Armstrongites are taught to interpret Scripture in the light of the writings of Herbert W. Armstrong. It is the common thing for a Worldwide Church of God lecturer, when citing prophecy concerning Israel, to pause and refer his auditors to *USBCP* for the identity of Israel and the key to prophecy. This is necessary because the Bible does not say that Anglo-Saxons are Israel. The cultish nature of Armstrongism is exposed in the fact that the basis of it can be, at best, an inference from Scripture. One does not grasp the key by reading the Bible: it is his only when he reads Armstrong! It is manifestly absurd to believe that for eighteen and one-half centuries the Word of God has been breathlessly anticipating the little 212-page book by Armstrong so that it could finally and actually become a revelation to man. Thus, anyone who takes Armstrong seriously in this is toying with blasphemy.

Armstrong makes Scripture dance to any tune he wishes to play. His followers are led to use Scripture as a

1 *USBCP*, p. 10.

gypsy fortune teller uses her deck of cards. They learn to shuffle Scripture and see Armstrongism, no matter what comes up. They see what they are told to see. The author recalls sitting next to a poor deluded fellow during an Armstrongite lecture. The man, waiting for the session to begin, earnestly explained how he had been examining prophecy and had seen significant prophetic connection between the cleansing of the sanctuary (Ezek. 45) and the cleansing of Peter's feet by Jesus. The man had been taught to see Armstrongism in the Bible. The Armstrongite methodology had him still seeing things.

An understanding of sound principles of Biblical interpretation will keep a man out of Armstrongism. As opposed to the many keys offered by a long line of false prophets, the following universally available, common sense principles of interpretation make God's propositional revelation open to all, without benefit of clergy.

1. Faith in Christ. If one rejects the Christ of the Scripture, he will be prejudiced in the choice of the meaning of words and significance of deeds and thoughts.[2]

2. Respect for the Bible as the Word of God. The question of the reliability of Scripture is one; the question of the meaning of Scripture is another. When one has settled the question, from available evidence, of the inspiration of Scripture, he is then in a position to correctly interpret the content of Scripture.

3. Harmonious with the whole. Truth is always consistent with truth. If a particular interpretation violates other parts of the revelation, then that interpretation is at fault.

4. Literal unless otherwise indicated. The inter-

---

[2] Lewis Foster, "Biblical Interpretation and Contemporary Thought," *The Restoration Herald* (Cincinnati, Ohio, May, 1968), pp. 12-13. The list of ten basic principles here is essentially the one detailed by Foster.

preter who wishes to read into a passage more of his own interests, will shy away from a literal treatment of the Bible. The duty of the interpreter is to determine the original intent of the author. A passage will be taken literally unless it, or portions of it, were not originally meant to be so understood.

5. Figurative if obvious. Because the Bible deals with things beyond human experience or comprehension, figurative or symbolic language is necessary.

6. Meaning from the context. The context may be adjoining verses, chapters, other Books, or the whole Bible itself. This principle is a preventative from "proof-texting."

7. Retention of the spirit. Words are simply vehicles to carry ideas. It is "letterism" and not "literalism" that destroys the spirit of the content of Scripture by loading more ideas upon the words than they were meant to carry.

8. Preserving the proper emphasis. A truth over-emphasized can easily become error. The content of divine revelation has proportion and balance. For instance, the emphasis of the Bible is upon Jesus Christ and the cross. The emphasis of Armstrongism is upon the "government of God."

9. Verification of interpretation. Nothing must be allowed to replace the Bible itself. But dictionaries, atlases, commentaries, introductions, background works, lexicons, and so forth, can contribute to each person's skill in Biblical interpretation.

10. Application to self. Without this, Biblical interpretation becomes mere academic exercise.

Beyond the solid principles of Biblical interpretation which apply to all kinds of Scriptural material, particular principles must be recognized in the handling of futuristic prophecy.

1. Prophecy can be infallibly interpreted only by an inspired interpreter. In I Corinthians 2:1-10 Paul affirms this principle.

2. It is not an issue of "literalism" versus "spiritualizing." The question is whether the original, intended meaning of a given prophecy has a temporal or spiritual fulfillment. If a prophecy has a spiritual meaning, then the spiritual or figurative application of it *is* a literal fulfillment.

3. If an inspired New Testament speaker or writer affirms that a certain prophecy is fulfilled in a certain way, that should settle the matter.

4. If Old or New Testament events have already fulfilled Old Testament prophecies, then those same prophecies cannot be changed to mean a future fulfillment.

5. If prophecies that *Scripture* links to certain events are not fulfilled in those events, then those events fulfill nothing.

6. To speak of the postponement of prophecy is nonsense. No prophecy can be taken centuries later to have a fulfillment in a way and at a time other than that which was intended when the prophecy was spoken or written. To say a fulfillment is deferred because of prevailing circumstances is to say that the prophecy is wrong,[3] and makes a false prophet out of the one making it. A prophecy cannot be wrong about time and right in every other detail. It deprives the prophecy of the element of inspiration. Prophecy then becomes mere prediction. If circumstances force the postponement of fulfillment, then there is no assurance that circumstances will permit fulfillment at a later time.

7. New Testament writers and speakers do not always quote the full prophecy or even quote verbatim. Often a paraphrase is used. Enough is given, however, so that one may know the source of the prophecy being explained.

[3] See Foy E. Wallace, Jr., *God's Prophetic Word* (Oklahoma City: Foy E. Wallace, Jr. Publications, 1960). Wallace enunciates sound principles in detail.

8. "Before His birth, and during the early part of His ministry, it was emphasized that Christ came to do a spiritual work, and that the cross was before Him *from the very beginning. Any theory of the interpretation of prophecy which does not take these two facts into consideration is unscriptural.*"[4]

This last principle is critical. It is decisive. It is Scriptural:

> Having therefore obtained help of God, I continue unto this day, witnessing both to small and great, saying none other things than those things which the prophets and Moses did say should come: That Christ should suffer, and that he should be the first that should rise from the dead, and should shew light unto the people, and to the Gentiles (Acts 26:22-23).

A particular principle applicable to promises made by the prophets to the northern kingdom before and after the fall of Samaria is this: *The destiny of Israel and the destiny of Judah are one. They are inseparably linked.* To seek a restoration of the house of Israel that is independent of the fortunes of the house of Judah is to ignore the main body of Old Testament prophecy. The link forged by the fiery spokesmen of God is an unbreakable one:

> And it shall come to pass, that as ye were a curse among the heathen, O house of Judah, and house of Israel; so will I save you, and ye shall be a blessing: fear not, but let your hands be strong (Zech. 8:13).

> And I will strengthen the house of Judah, and I will save the house of Joseph, and I will bring them again to place them; for I have mercy upon them: and they shall be as though I had not cast them off: for I am the LORD their God (Zech. 10:6).

[4] James D. Bales, *The New Testament Interpretation of Old Testament Prophecies of the Kingdom* (Searcy, Ark.: Harding College Press, 1950) p. 1.

> And in those days the house of Judah shall
> walk with the house of Israel, and they shall
> come together out of the land of the north to the
> land that I have given for an inheritance unto
> your fathers (Jer. 3:18).

The famous scene in Ezekiel 37:15 ff. of the joining of the two sticks in the hand of the prophet—one stick for Judah, one for Israel—into one stick, settles this point. Without multiplying examples *ad taedeum*, it should be incontrovertible that whatever happens to one is the equal destiny of the other.

Another principle of interpretation that directly affects Old Testament material and the understanding of it concerns the issue of the literary form of modern formal logic versus the literary form of the pre-Aristotle, proto-logical period. Little work has been done in this area by experts in the field of hermeneutics. The term "proto-logical" was coined by the world's leading Ancient Near Eastern linguist, William Foxwell Albright. His pioneer and definitive work in this area is the most complete explanation of the principle.[5] The thrust of his work is corroborative. He points out that liberal scholars have no basis for dating the patriarchal narratives later than the fourteenth century B.C. He demonstrates that the literary form reflects that of the time of Moses and Joshua.

Keep in mind that the inspiration of all Scripture has to do with content, not the literary form in which the content is expressed. Isaiah and Matthew agree in fact and doctrine, but they do not express truth in identical literary styles.

In the area of content, Albright faults modern critics for imposing the thought patterns of modern formal logic on the patriarchal narratives and the writings of the prophets. The literary form of the Old

[5] William F. Albright, *History, Archaeology, and Christian Humanism* (New York: McGraw Hill Book Co., 1964).

Testament is of the time before Thales and Aristotle. Pre-Aristotelian logic was a logic of common sense and experience. (This kind of logic is actually more reliable than formal logic.) The literary form of the ancient Biblical documents does not reflect the preciseness and exclusiveness of syllogistic thinking. It was not pre-logical; it was simply a different working of logical processes.

When working with Old Testament texts, we must take care not to insist that certain words, phrases, idioms, figures, and so forth, mean exactly what they would mean if we ourselves had written them. In other words, we must read Moses in the literary context of Moses, instead of projecting upon him the linguistic nuances of a later literary context.

An example of Armstrong's system of interpretation is here examined:

To Spread Worldwide

> And again in Genesis 28:13-14, where the added detail that these nations of Israel shall eventually spread around the world is recorded. "And behold the ETERNAL ... said, 'I am the ETERNAL God of Abraham thy father, and the God of Isaac: the land whereon thou liest, to thee will I give it, and to thy seed; And thy seed shall be as the dust of the earth, and thou shalt spread abroad to the west, and to the east, and to the north, and to the south. . . .'"

> The original Hebrew for "spread abroad" means "to break forth." This promise places *no limit* on *how far* east, west, north and south Jacob's descendants should spread. Thus it indicates that they would spread around the earth. This is confirmed in Romans 4:13: "For the promise, that he (Abraham) should be the heir of the world. . . ."[6]

By the simple expediency of making "spread abroad"

6 *USBCP*, pp. 28, 29.

mean what he (Armstrong) wants it to mean—that is, "around the earth"—"the land whereon thou liest" becomes "the globe whereon thou liest." He then quotes just enough of Romans 4:13 to give the impression that Paul confirms his interpretation. But one must be careful not to read the entire verse, for it is:

> For the promise, that he should be the heir of the world, was not to Abraham, or to his seed, through the law, but through the righteousness of faith.

The obvious meaning of Romans 4:13 is that the promise to Abraham that he would be heir of the world was not realized in his physical descendants, but in his spiritual seed through faith in Christ (Gal. 3:29). By quoting a part of a verse and lifting it from context Armstrong "confirms" a proposition that is *the opposite* of what the text cited actually teaches.

In the next paragraph, he continues:

> Yet, in the new earth—after the millennium—Romans 4:13 shows the earth will be inhabited *only* by those who shall be Abraham's children *through* CHRIST.[7]

As if the first deception were not enough, he then reverses himself, arbitrarily shifts the emphasis of Romans 4:13 to the future (which is not mentioned in Romans 4), and declares that it also teaches global occupation by the spiritual seed. Thus the clear meaning of the verse—that now any individual in Christ is "Abraham's seed and heir according to the promise"—is carefully avoided. By juggling words to give the impression that Romans 4:13 teaches both the physical and spiritual inheritance of the world by Abraham, Armstrong seeks to preserve the myth that God promised to Abraham and Jacob imperial glory. The convenience of Armstrongite Biblical interpretation is apparent. If

[7] *Ibid.*

Romans 4 is fulfilled in both flesh and faith, then the Bible is not a propositional revelation, but a crystal ball. The prerequisite for believing this contradictory confusion is a blind belief in Armstrong himself.

The Armstrongite cry "It's in your Bible" will become the death knell of the cult when people begin to read the Bible without Herbert W. Armstrong looking over the shoulder. He hurries them past much Scripture so he can tell them how to read other Scripture. He then assures them that they did not get it from him but from God.

Parenthetically it should be noted that God promised to Abraham the land of Canaan, and this promise was fulfilled in the period of conquest under Joshua:

> And the LORD gave unto Israel all the land which he sware to give unto their fathers; and they possessed it, and dwelt therein. And the LORD gave them rest round about, according to all that he sware unto their fathers: and there stood not a man of all their enemies before them; the LORD delivered all their enemies into their hand. There failed not aught of any good thing which the LORD had spoken unto the House of Israel; all came to pass (Josh. 21:43-45).

God's land promise to the patriarchs has been declared fulfilled by Scripture. The only land promise yet unkept is the one made by Herbert W. Armstrong.

4 THE HOPE OF ISRAEL

The interest in discovering a Lost Israel is generated by a conviction of the prophetic necessity of doing so. If the promises of God are to be fulfilled in an ethnic Israel, then an ethnic Israel must be available for future fulfillment of prophecy. Thus far God has shown little interest in the racial aspirations of man. Armstrong makes available to God the royal family of England and the Anglo-Saxon peoples. They are holding the throne of David in trust for Christ.

What is the "hope of Israel"? Whatever it is, or was, the Jews of the first century were wrong about it. The record is clear that the Jewish system of Biblical interpretation caused them to miss their Messiah. If we use the same methodology, we shall be as confounded as they.

Paul, before Agrippa, urging the claims of Christ, said:

> And now I stand and am judged for the hope of the promise made of God unto our fathers: Unto which promise our twelve tribes, instantly serving God day and night, hope to come. For which hope's sake, king Agrippa, I am accused of the Jews (Acts 26:6-7).

And in the presence of the chief Jews of Rome:

> For this cause therefore have I called for you, to see you, and to speak with you: because

that for the hope of Israel I am bound with this chain (Acts 28:20).

The first-century Jewish concept of the hope of Israel was wrong. Their false hope crucified Jesus, stoned Stephen, and had Paul in chains.

The Jews were convinced that the Old Testament taught a hope of Israel to be realized in a Messiah on a temporal throne over a temporal kingdom, with preferential treatment for Israel. They were wrong. Armstrong teaches that the hope of Israel is a Messiah on a temporal throne over a temporal kingdom. Armstrong is wrong. He is preaching the doctrine that drove the nails into the hands of the Master.

The hope that Jesus brought to Israel was not the hope that they hoped for. That generation of Jews did not hate Jesus because He promised no earthly kingdom to *them*; they hated Him because He promised no earthly kingdom *at all*. "My kingdom is not of this world," declared Jesus (John 18:36). The theology of the New Testament is salvation by grace. Armstrong sees the promises fulfilled in race. So did the Jews who rejected Jesus. The dispensational view of Old Testament prophecy is precisely the view held by the generation of Jews to whom Jesus preached.

The Land Promise to the Patriarchs

Armstrongite materialism insists that the hope of Israel includes real estate. The question is very simple. Either the land promised to Abraham and Jacob has been given to their descendants or it has not. If it has not been, then Armstrong has gained some "ground." If the land promise has been kept, then Armstrong is wrong; and the "ground" is cut from under his theological system.

God Promised the Larger Boundaries

Moses recorded in the Book of Exodus that God

had promised the gradual elimination of the many Canaanite tribes:

> By little and little I will drive them out from before thee, until thou be increased, and inherit the land. And I will set thy bounds from the Red sea even unto the sea of the Philistines, and from the desert unto the river: for I will deliver the inhabitants of the land into your hand; and thou shalt drive them out before thee (Exod. 23:30-31).

It is immaterial whether the "river of Egypt" (Num. 34:5), constituting the southwestern boundary of the promised land, was the Nile or the *Wady el-'Arish*, a stream east of the Nile. The country between the stream and the Nile was mainly desert. The Nile was virtually on the boundary of Egypt. The passage means that the descendants of Abraham should possess the land as far as the borders of Egypt, not Egypt itself. However, because dispensationalists see fit to scoff at the *Wady el-'Arish* as a candidate for the title "river of Egypt," it should be noted that the weight of evidence is in the favor of this identification. It is not sound Biblical interpretation to project upon Moses both modern geography and geology. There is little, if any, Scriptural or archaeological evidence that the River of Egypt, when spoken of as a boundary of the promised land, is the Nile. J. A. Selbie says of the River of Egypt:

> It is not the Nile but the *Wady el-'Arish*, which flows through the northern portion of the Sinaitic peninsula, draining into itself the waters of many other wadies, and flows into the Mediterranean midway between Pelusium and Gaza.[1]

This fits with the promise of God that the southwestern boundary would run a line "from the Red sea even unto the sea of the Philistines" (Exod. 23:31).

[1] "River of Egypt," *The Popular and Critical Bible Encyclopedia* (2nd ed.), I, 577.

Israel Occupied the Inheritance

At the end of the forty years of wandering, Moses, in his farewell address, recalls that he had given them the go-ahead to claim the promise of God:

> Behold, I have set the land before you: go in and possess the land which the LORD sware unto your fathers, Abraham, Isaac, and Jacob, to give unto them and to their seed (Deut. 1:8).

After the conquest was accomplished, "Joshua let the people depart, every man unto his inheritance" (Josh. 24:28).

The Inheritance Temporary and Conditional

The inheritance of Israel of a land with houses they had not built and wells they had not dug was accompanied with both warnings and gloomy predictions. Possession of the land depended upon fidelity to God. The dying Joshua said to a people already turning away from God:

> Therefore it shall come to pass, that as all good things are come upon you, which the LORD your God promised you; so shall the LORD bring upon you all evil things, until he have destroyed you from off this good land which the LORD your God hath given you. When ye have transgressed the covenant of the LORD your God, which he commanded you, and have gone and served other gods, and bowed yourselves to them; then shall the anger of the LORD be kindled against you, and ye shall perish quickly from off the good land which he hath given unto you (Josh. 23:15-16).

The Heathen Not Driven Out

Because Israel preferred cohabitation with the people of the land rather than paying the price of driving them out, as God had commanded, the covenant people forfeited their right to retain their possession:

And the anger of the LORD was hot against Israel; and he said, Because that this people hath transgressed my covenant which I commanded their fathers, and have not hearkened unto voice; I also will not henceforth drive out any from before them of the nations which Joshua left when he died: That through them I may prove Israel, whether they will keep the way of the LORD to walk therein, as their fathers did keep it, or not. Therefore the LORD left those nations, without driving them out hastily; neither delivered he them into the hand of Joshua (Judges 2:20-23).

The pagan altars were left standing, and Israel lost control of a portion of the land.

The Promise Declared Fulfilled

Armstrong notwithstanding, Joshua declared that the land promise made to Abraham had been fulfilled:

And the LORD gave unto Israel all the land which he sware to give unto their fathers; and they possessed it, and dwelt therein (21:43).

There failed not aught of any good thing which the LORD had spoken unto the house of Israel; all came to pass (21:45).

And, behold, this day I am going the way of all the earth: and ye know in all your hearts and in all your souls, that not one thing hath failed of all the good things which the LORD your God spake concerning you; all are come to pass unto you, and not one thing hath failed thereof (23:14).

That the promise has been fulfilled is confirmed by Nehemiah:

Thou art the LORD the God, who didst choose Abram, and broughtest him forth out of Ur of the Chaldees, and gavest him the name of Abraham; And foundest his heart faithful before thee, and madest a covenant with him to give the land of the Canaanites, the Hittites, the Amorites, and the Perizzites, and the Jebusites, and the Girgashites, to give it, I say, to his seed, and hast performed thy words; for thou art righteous (9:7-8).

The narration of Stephen in Acts 7 includes the information that the promise made to Abraham concerning land was fulfilled with the Exodus and the period of conquest. He said,

But when the time of the promise drew nigh, which God had sworn to Abraham, the people grew and multiplied in Egypt (7:17).

Joshua, Nehemiah, and Stephen agree that the word of God to His servant and friend Abraham concerning the land that He would give to His heirs has been vindicated. Armstrong says that it has not been. Someone is wrong.

David Recovered It

The campaigns of David against the Philistines and the Moabites and the Syrians accomplished the recovery of the land lost to Israel in the apostasy of the nation. The record is that

David smote also Hadadezer, the son of Rehob, king of Zobah, as he went to recover his border at the river Euphrates (II Sam. 8:3).

Solomon Ruled over It

The larger land of Canaan was a part of the Solomonic kingdom. Even if the original conquest had not fulfilled the promise, as Scripture declares it did, the promise would have been kept in the days of David and Solomon. The inspired history is:

And Solomon reigned over all kingdoms from the river unto the land of the Philistines, and unto the border of Egypt: they brought

> presents, and served Solomon all the days of his
> life (I Kings 4:21).

> For he had dominion over all the region on
> this side the river, from Tiphsah even to Azzah
> [Gaza], over all the kings on this side the river:
> and he had peace on all sides round about him.
> And Judah and Israel dwelt safely, every man
> under his vine and under his fig tree, from Dan
> even to Beer-sheba, all the days of Solomon (I
> Kings 4:24-25).

The Biblical record is clear that the land promise to
Abraham has been kept. If the promises made to Abraham are yet anticipating fulfillment, then the inspired
writers erred in agreeing that God has already kept His
word. The claim by Joshua that "not one thing hath
failed thereof" (23:14) settles it.

Restoration Prophecies

The yet-puzzled disciples of Jesus stood with Him
upon the Mount of Ascension and asked, "Lord, wilt
thou at this time restore again the kingdom to Israel?"
(Acts 1:6). The promise that "Loammi" would be restored to the favor of God has been the hope of Israel:

> Yet the number of the children of Israel
> shall be as the sand of the sea, which cannot be
> measured nor numbered; and it shall come to
> pass, that in the place where it was said unto
> them, Ye are not my people, there it shall be said
> unto them, Ye are the sons of the living God
> (Hos. 1:10).

If this promise means political and national restoration of Israel, if it is meant to be taken "literally," then
Israel must be available for the regathering into a political entity. If it is to be understood spiritually, then the
existence of Lost Tribes or a nation of Jews is of no
consequence.

Return Versus Restoration

The dispensational cry that the affirmation of a

non-imperial, spiritual fulfillment of the prophecies of the hope of Israel is "spiritualizing away the promises" must be examined. Armstrong cannot "have his cake and eat it too." Either the hope of Israel is in a temporal restoration or it is not. To restore the kingdom would logically mean not only the return to the land, but a reestablishment of the royal line upon the throne, the political order, the laws, the original land allotments, and the Mosaic religion. This proposition does not require proof because it is generally accepted by all brands of dispensationalists. Armstrong affirms that "after the coming of Christ to rule, it is evident that Israel is again to offer sacrifices, burnt offerings and meat offerings."[2]

Israel was promised a national *return*. The "Israel" that was removed walked back with Judah "out of the land of the north" (Jer. 3:18). Chapter 2 of this work cites Scriptural proof that the dedication of the Temple was by twelve-tribed Israel. Mosaic religion was again practiced. But the restoration of the political structure of the northern kingdom was denied Israel. The promise had been that if Israel did not fear God, He would "destroy thee from off the face of the earth" (Deut. 6:15):

> And it shall be, if thou do at all forget the LORD thy God, and walk after other gods, and serve them, and worship them, I testify against you this day that ye shall surely perish. As the nations which the LORD destroyed before your face, so shall ye perish; because ye would not be obedient unto the voice of the LORD your God (Deut. 8:19-20).

The conditions were enforced (Jer. 18:1-10). Moses warned of it (Deut. 30:17-18). Joshua said they would lose their inheritance (Josh. 23:13).

The ultimate restoration of Israel was to be spiritu-

2 *USBCP*, p. 73.

al. Armstrong admits that complete national restoration requires the rebuilding of the Temple and the reinstitution of Jewish ceremonialism and ordinances—in short, a return to Moses. This would be a bringing back into force of those things that foreshadowed the gospel. The shadow (Col. 2:17) would replace the substance. That which Jesus nailed to His cross (Col. 2:14) would be taken down from the cross and put back in authority. Men would regress from faith back to the tutelage of the schoolmaster (Gal. 3:25). The son would once again become the bondservant (Gal. 4:7). The perfect covenant would be filed away and the faulty one observed (Heb. 8:7). Jerusalem would answer to Sinai (Gal. 4:25). All men would become debtor to do the whole Law and would be "fallen from grace" (Gal. 5:3-4). This absurd interpretation of Scripture is based upon the old Jewish presupposition of a temporal hope for Israel, and can survive only if the proponent thereof carefully avoids reading the New Testament. Armstrong teaches that selected portions of the Law are to be kept now, and the remainder will be kept in the millennium. No wonder he seldom directs the attention of the reader of *USBCP* to the New Testament.

Loammi and Ammi

Hosea promised that when Loammi ("not my people") became Ammi ("my people"), this would be the time when both the children of Judah and the children of Israel would be gathered together under one head (1:10-11). Either this has happened or it has not. If the New Testament produces an inspired interpretation of this promise, and thereby of duplicate promises, then no more room remains for speculation. In the Book of Romans Paul cites this prophecy:

> ... Even us, whom he hath called, not of the Jews only, but also of the Gentiles? As he saith also in Osee, I will call them my people, which were not my people; and her beloved, which was

99

not beloved. And it shall come to pass, that in the place where it was said unto them, Ye are not my people; there shall they be called the children of the living God (Rom. 9:24-26).

And then citing what he considers to be the companion prophecy (Isa. 10:22-23), Paul continues:

"Esaias also crieth concerning Israel, Though the number of the children of Israel be as the sand of the sea, a remnant shall be saved" (9:27).

The apostle cites these texts as prophetic proof that God all along planned to include the Gentiles in His restoration program (9:24). The thrust of Romans 9 is that all the seed of Abraham are not the children of the promise, and that the original intended meaning of the restoration promise was that the gathering, mentioned in Hosea 1, was to be of Gentiles and Jews together into *the church*. If the meaning of the promise of Hosea is that Israel is to join Judah in a future national restoration of the theocratic kingdom, then Paul erred grievously in introducing the text into his argument. He is absolutely not speaking of the future nor of any supposed millennial reign of Jesus. The meaning of the prophecy is clear. When God proclaimed apostate Israel "Loammi," He meant exactly that. They became "not his people"; that is, they became Gentile. They can be restored, and the remnant can be saved, but it must be by obeying the gospel and becoming a part of the "Israel of God" (Gal. 6:16), the church.

If this is the intended meaning of both the Hosea and the Isaiah texts, then it fits perfectly and precisely into the argument of Romans 9 and 10. If this is not the intended meaning, if the dispensationalists are correct that the church is some kind of parenthetical mystery and the hope of Israel in restoration has nothing to do with the fact that the gospel was for the Gentiles as well as for the Jews, then the citation of the texts as proof by Paul is meaningless.

The Jews believed in salvation by race, and rejected Jesus when He refused to go along. Jesus brought the plan of grace. Armstrong agrees with the Jews. In a section captioned "Race, Not Grace," he asserts that "Sceptre" promises culminated in Christ and the church, but "Birthright" promises were reserved for "Israel," that is, Anglo-Saxons. He says, "But the astonishing truth is that the Birthright promises were never given to the Jews!"[3]

If the New Testament does not teach that the distinction between Jew and Gentile has been dissolved in Christ, then it teaches nothing at all:

> That at that time ye [Gentiles] were without Christ, being aliens from the commonwealth of Israel, and strangers from the covenants of promise, having no hope, and without God in the world: But now in Christ Jesus ye who sometimes were far off are made nigh by the blood of Christ. For he is our peace, who hath made both one, and hath broken down the middle wall of partition between us; Having abolished in his flesh the enmity, even the law of commandments contained in ordinances; for to make in himself of twain one new man, so making peace (Eph. 2:12-15).

> There is neither Jew nor Greek, there is neither bond nor free, there is neither male nor female: for ye are all one in Christ Jesus (Gal. 3:28).

It is a "new Galatianism" that a man must obey not only the gospel, but the law of Moses as well to be saved. It is the old Jewish error resurrected that "restored Israel" shall be a gathering of Jews or Israel as opposed to Gentiles. The basic point of Romans 9—11 is that the commonwealth of Israel is a spiritual body

3 *Ibid.*, p. 35.

made up of all—both Jew and Gentile—who obey the gospel. The eleventh chapter of Romans affirms that "so all Israel shall be saved" (v. 26). The Armstrongite interpretation of that statement is that when the hope of Israel is realized, not only will world-rule be the portion of Israel, but also a special opportunity for salvation. If that is the correct interpretation of verse 26, then Paul is giving a conclusion of the argument running from Romans 9—11 that denies the truth of the argument itself. He says that "they are not all Israel, which are of Israel"; that is, the promises of God of the hope of Israel have never meant salvation by race or because of race. All are "concluded . . . in unbelief, that he might have mercy upon all" (11:32). "For there is no difference between the Jew and the Greek," he continues; "for whosoever shall call upon the name of the Lord shall be saved" (10:12-13).

The argument is that God is not faithless because most of the Jews failed to become heirs of the promises. He points out that God kept His new covenant promises in the establishing of the church. And if the Jews are going to be a part of restored Israel, they are going to have to obey the gospel. This is what verse 26 teaches. The word *outōs*, "so," is used as an adverb of manner. *In that way*—that is, by obeying the gospel—shall all Israel have to be saved, if they are going to be saved. If this is the meaning of the statement, then it is in perfect harmony with the context. If this is not the meaning, then conclusion contradicts proposition.

The dispensational or "literal" interpretation of Romans 11:26 does not make sense, even in the dispensational context. The wildest, most fanciful, most imaginative of dispensational schemes does not provide for the salvation of *all* Israel. Those who have died and shall die before the supposed millennial reign of Christ will be lost unless they have turned to Christ in faith. Even all those who witness the return of Christ and the rapture of the church will not necessarily qualify.

The very ones who cry for "literalism" in interpreting prophecy must shrink back into the figurative or spiritual in the face of this verse, or else find themselves affirming that the accident of birth which produces an Israelite also produces a saint.

The answer to the question of salvation by race or salvation by grace is, "And if ye be Christ's, then are ye Abraham's seed, and heirs according to the promise" (Gal. 3:29).

Armstrong has fallen into the ancient error of supposing that Israel is still the chosen race. Israel was chosen to bring the knowledge of sin to the world through the Law of Moses (Rom. 3:20). Israel was chosen to bring the Savior to the world. This has been done. Israel isn't chosen anymore.

The chosen-race concept has been subverted into a master-race concept. The old Jewish error was not really chosen-racism, but master-racism. Israel was chosen to be a blessing (Gen. 12:2). This blessing in Christ was to be a spiritual blessing. Israel never was set apart as a master race. Armstrongism is master-racism under the guise of chosen-racism. It has always been so disguised.

There have been many kinds of master-racism, but the practical results have always been the same. Master-racism has always appealed to the baser of man's instincts. Armstrongism is no exception.

The Ku Klux Klan and its dream of a Protestant empire sees WASPS (White Anglo-Saxon Protestants) as the chosen race. It is nothing more than the kind of master-racism that Hitler preached and it has often been associated with it. This chosen-racism has been offered as the theological justification for the American system of slavery and segregation.

The white man often spoke of America as the "promised land" and saw himself as the "chosen" to make a conquest of it. Thus the Indian heathen could be dismissed as a subject of the kind of wrath God visited upon ancient Canaan.

103

The Dutch established the first European settlement at the Cape of South Africa in 1652. To operate the settlement, they introduced black slavery into the early history of the continent. Later the Cape fell to British dominion. The Dutch, unhappy with British rule, moved northward in what has been called "The Great Trek" in 1835. The familiar wagon train circled at night against roaming tribes of African people. The settlers had daily devotions and saw themselves as the people of God in search of a "promised land." Indeed, the Dutch Voortrekkers looked upon themselves as "God's Chosen People." They compared their trek to that of the Israelites as they marched through Sinai toward Canaan. They set out to destroy the heathen tribes. The Dutch trekboers (farmers) marched across the land and in the name of God murdered the Bantu and other tribes. This religious concept laid the foundation for the present political and social concept of "apartheid" or separate development, whereby the white race is held to be superior and has every right to rule and subjugate the black.

With the same theology England subjugated a world of nonwhites.

On and on goes the story. Armstrong takes his chosen-race doctrine and logically holds for strict segregation of races. He teaches the old Jewish error that Israel is chosen of God for preferential treatment and privilege. He makes God a respecter of persons. Armstrongism has the stench of Buchenwald. It glows with the brilliance of the Klansman's burning cross. It nods its approval as the white man piously plunders in the name of religion. It blasphemes the God who has "made of one blood all nations of men" (Acts 17:26). Armstrongism will prosper because corrupted man has always wanted to believe that kind of thing anyway.

The Tabernacle of David

All brands of dispensationalism, Armstrongism included, see Amos 9:11-12 as key verses. It is labeled "future kingdom blessing" and is linked to the reestablishment of the Davidic monarchy and throne. Critical, then, is the use of it in the Book of Acts. The scene in Acts 15 was the Jerusalem conference on circumcision. Testimony is received by the apostles and elders of the experience of Peter in the house of Cornelius. Barnabas and Paul told how God had worked miracles and wonders among the Gentiles (Acts 15:12). Then the half-brother of Jesus stands to speak:

> Simeon hath declared how God at the first did visit the Gentiles, to take out of them a people for his name. And to this agree the words of the prophets; as it is written, After this I will return, and will build again the tabernacle of David, which is fallen down; and I will build again the ruins thereof, and I will set it up: That the residue of men might seek after the Lord, and all the Gentiles, upon whom my name is called, saith the Lord, who doeth all these things (Acts 15:14-17; cf. Amos 9:11-12).

Armstrong claims that the tabernacle of David will be set up when the throne of David is set up, at the Second Coming. The problem with this is that James says absolutely nothing about the Second Coming of the Lord. The debate among the Jewish Christians was about whether or not the Gentiles, who had already begun to obey the gospel, were proper candidates for the church. James cites the testimony of Peter that God had instigated the program of Gentile evangelism; and he asserts, under the inspiration of the Holy Spirit, that there was prophetic justification, quoting Amos. The return of the Lord had nothing whatever to do with the subject under discussion.

The plain meaning is that God *had already* set up the tabernacle of David—that is the church—so the Gentiles could seek Him. And they can seek Him now in an acceptable way because the tabernacle of David has been set up. To project this Old Testament prophecy into the future, to a time when God would call the Gentiles to a participation in Mosaic ceremonialism, is to subvert the text as it appears in the context. The citation is made by James to prove that God *was already* including the Gentiles in His restoration plans and to prove that the Gentiles did not have to become Jewish proselytes before becoming eligible for obedience to the gospel. In other words, the prophecy did not include Gentiles in the Jewish economy: it *excluded them from Jewish legal requirements.* Armstrong teaches the *opposite;* that is, that the prophecy looks forward to a future rebuilding of the Temple and the participation of Gentiles in Jewish ceremonial worship.

In the connection in which James uses this prophecy, if it is not fulfilled, then all Gentiles are still lost.

The Throne of David

It is demonstrated in this section that the kingdom of God promised to both Israel and Judah is the church and that Christ as the Head of the church is now reigning upon the throne of David. This being true, it cannot be defended that the throne of David will be established at the return of Jesus, either in Jerusalem or in London (as traditional British-Israelism teaches).

The expectations of national restoration and the hope of Israel are linked to the throne and kingdom promises. The logical connection is made in prophecy between kingdom territory and the reign of the king.

The Sure Mercies of David

The prophecy of the "sure mercies of David" is recorded in II Samuel 7:11-16. God declared through Nathan that David will not be permitted to build a house for God. The task will fall to Solomon. But David should find comfort in the promise that God was going to build a "house" for him. He would raise up one of the seed of

David to occupy the throne. The account of the promise includes assurance that (a) one of the seed of David will receive a kingdom (v. 12), (b) it will be done while David is in the grave (v. 12), (c) he will suffer at the hands of men (v. 14), and (d) the mercy of God will not depart from him as it did from Saul (v. 15). Because of this last part of the prophecy, that of mercy not-to-be-withdrawn, the name of the promise came to be "the sure mercies of David" (Isa. 55:3; Ps. 89:28-29).

Either this prophecy has been fulfilled or it has not been. If it has been fulfilled, Armstrong suffers a wound in the body of the World Church of God theology that is unquestionably fatal.

Armstrong teaches that "Jesus Christ will not sit upon the throne of David until His Second Coming to earth, yet future!"[4] He understands the "sure mercies" portion of the Davidic Covenant to mean that Solomon's dynasty would never end;[5] therefore the royal line of David must have existed in the flesh, somewhere, until now. Therefore the "sure mercies" cannot have been fulfilled in any spiritual way.

British-Israelism—Armstrongism attempts to have the Davidic line survive in the flesh through Zedekiah, who was not even in line for that honor. Ezekiel denounces him as a "prince of Nebuchadnezzar" and renounces him as Davidic king (21:25-27). Armstrong tampers with the Biblical genealogy (Luke 3 and Matt. 1); he omits Jehoiachin (variants: Jeconiah, Coniah), and inserts Zedekiah. This is done to connect Zedekiah's daughter with the royal throne of Judah.

He then confuses Jeremiahs (there are eight besides the prophet). He has the prophet being the father of Hamutal, therefore the grandfather of Zedekiah. But the Scriptures distinguish between the two by naming the grandfather of Zedekiah "Jeremiah of Libnah" (II Kings

4 *Ibid.*, p. 69.
5 *Ibid.*, p. 68.

23:31; 24:18; Jer. 52:1) to avoid confusing him with Jeremiah (the prophet) of Anathoth (Jer. 1:1). The prophet was of the family line of "priests"—that is, Levites—and therefore could not be a part of the house of Judah.

As a parenthetical note concerning the fleshly (Anglo-Saxon) fulfillment of the "sure mercies" promise through the royal house of England through Zedekiah, it should be observed that there is more Teutonic blood in Queen Elizabeth than there is Saxon blood. (The Saxons themselves are a mixture of Normans, Picts, Celts, Gauls, and German Teutons.) The house of Este (Italian) married into the houses of Brunswick and Hanover, from which descended the British line of sovereignty. The house of Hanover is German. During World War I England changed the name to the house of Brunswick, but the fact remains that the line is mixed with Italian and German to a predominant extent. And if the throne of England is the throne of David, then America has perpetuated a rebellion against the divine throne of God upon earth. Logically, we should recant the Declaration of Independence and once again subject ourselves to the royal line of England.

It is foolish anyway to argue on the basis of "sure mercies" for constant occupation of the throne. Hosea warned:

> For the children of Israel shall abide many days without a king, and without a prince, and without a sacrifice, and without an image, and without an ephod, and without teraphim (3:4).

The matter of the meaning of the "sure mercies" promise is settled by Paul in his sermon at Antioch, recorded in Acts 13. The subject is the resurrection of Jesus:

> But God raised him from the dead: And he was seen many days of them which came up with him from Galilee to Jerusalem, who are his wit-

nesses unto the people. And we declare unto you glad tidings, how that the promise which was made unto the fathers, *God hath fulfilled* the same unto us their children, in that he hath raised up Jesus again; as it is also written in the second psalm, Thou art my Son, this day have I begotten thee. And as concerning that he raised him up from the dead, now no more to return to corruption, he said on this wise, I will give you the sure mercies of David (vv. 30-34).

This statement of fulfilled prophecy contains two decisive declarations. God has fulfilled two promises, both of which are held to be key dispensational prophecies: the second Psalm ("rod of iron") and the "sure mercies of David." He has fulfilled them *in that* He raised Jesus from the dead. Armstrong and others deny both counts. Armstrongism demands that the fulfillment of these prophecies be reserved for the future. The fulfillment must be in the Second Coming and not the resurrection of Jesus. In perfect harmony with the use by Paul is the citation of the II Samuel passage by Peter at Pentecost:

Men and brethren, let me freely speak unto you of the patriarch David, that he is both dead and buried, and his sepulchre is with us unto this day. Therefore being a prophet, and knowing that God has sworn with an oath to him, that of the fruit of his loins, according to the flesh, he would raise up Christ to sit on his throne; He seeing this before *spake of the resurrection of Christ,* that his soul was not left in hell, neither his flesh did see corruption. This Jesus hath God raised up, whereof we are all witnesses. Therefore being by the right hand of God exalted, and having received of the Father the promise of the Holy Ghost, he hath shed forth this, which ye now see and hear (Acts 2:29-33).

Devastating to all brands of dispensationalism are the following points in the above passage: (*a*) the resurrection of Jesus fulfilled the part of the promise that the throne would be established while David was in the grave (this could not be true in the dispensational view that the throne is established *after* the resurrection of the just); (*b*) "seeing" the promise before, he spoke of the resurrection of Christ, not the Second Coming; (*c*) the throne of David is now occupied by Jesus as He is exalted at the right hand of God.

Jesus is reigning upon a throne now (Heb. 1:3-13). He has all authority. There is not a scrap of authority that Armstrong can assign to Jesus in a millennium that the New Testament does not affirm that He enjoys now. Has Jesus been reigning for almost two thousand years upon a throne about which prophecy is silent?

The contention which both the Jews and Armstrong have had with the New Testament writers is that the throne must be temporal. The reign must be corporeal. The old Jewish error, perpetuated by Armstrong, rejects the concept of the rule of God in corporeal absentia, which rule is through a divine revelation. That is the kind of rule Christ now has over the church. That was the kind of rule God had over Israel through the period of the Judges. The theocracy made God the King over Israel, without benefit of an earthly throne. When Israel insisted upon the kind of king they could see, God made it plain that the demand constituted a rejection of Himself (I Sam. 8:7). The royal throne of Israel was established by God reluctantly and in His wrath. Armstrongism shrugs off the rule of Christ through the New Testament as relatively unimportant. He cries out for a temporal throne. He cries out for the kind of throne that God established in His wrath. He cries out for the kind of throne the Jews wanted but Jesus refused to give them. He cries out for the kind of rule that God did not want and did not promise. How hollow rings his pious claim that he is preaching the same gospel Jesus preached. He is preaching the faith of Judas!

110

The second Psalm is a banner waved by Armstrong and the hosts of interdenominational dispensationalists as classic proof of the millennial reign of Jesus on earth in the future:

> Yet I have set my king upon my holy hill of Zion. I will declare the decree: the LORD hath said unto me, thou art my Son; this day have I begotten thee. Ask of me, and I shall give thee the heathen for thine inheritance, and the uttermost parts of the earth for thy possession. Thou shalt break them with a rod of iron; thou shalt dash them in pieces like a potter's vessel (vv. 6-9).

This psalm is cited in the sermon of Paul (Acts 13:30-34), as has already been indicated. It is cited there as prophetic evidence of the resurrection of Jesus. The first part of the psalm was sung by the early church as they celebrated the release of Peter and John from punishment (Acts 4:23-25). It is cited in Hebrews 1:1-5 in an expression of praise to Christ in His *present reign*. It is used only once with any connection to the Second Coming, and this use is fatal to Armstrongite doctrine:

> But that which ye have already hold fast till I come. And he that overcometh, and keepeth my works unto the end, to him will I give power over the nations: And he shall rule them with a rod of iron; as the vessels of a potter shall they be broken to shivers: *even as I received of my Father* (Rev. 2:25-27).

The text is clear. The promise to the endangered Christians at Thyatira was that if they would remain faithful, they would share in the reign which Jesus had *already received*. The use of the second Psalm here is perfectly

111

consistent with the other citations of it in the New Testament.

To literalize the expression "rod of iron" into a picture of the Master forcing His rule upon a reluctant race during a millennial period is to have God violate the free-will principle that permitted the Fall and instigated the cross. Unless God miraculously transformed the heart of man, the rod of iron reign upon earth over living men would be a global prison system and not utopia.

The rod of iron figure does not mean political and temporal. It means strong and complete. As a matter of fact, the strongest and most complete sovereignty enjoyed by any king is spiritual. A temporal king can rule the bodies of men only insofar as he can reign in the hearts of men. When he no longer enjoys the voluntary subservience of his subjects, he soon loses his throne. This is to say that the kind of rule Jesus has over His church now is the strongest and most complete rule there can be. A system of rule established by the intimidating power of a coming Christ would be an inferior dominion. The Biblical picture of the return of Jesus is of one judging and destroying those who despised His rule.

The Kingdom

One of the problems in dealing with the kingdom is the fact that the term does not enjoy a perfectly consistent use in Scripture. This section demonstrates that the kingdom, insofar as it is synonymous with the hope of Israel in restoration, new covenant, and throne of David, is the church. This in no way contradicts the fact that the term sometimes refers to the future bliss of the believer and sometimes to the rule of God in the human heart in a general way.

The time of the kingdom. The key prophecies of the kingdom that focus upon the time of the setting up of the reign of Messiah are found in the Book of Daniel.

Nebuchadnezzar and Daniel had companion visions in their respective dreams of the great image and the four beasts. The dream of the king was of the image thus described:

> This image's head was of fine gold, his breast and his arms of silver, his belly and his thighs of brass, His legs of iron, his feet part of iron and part of clay (Dan. 2:32-33).

A stone cut out of the mountain, not with human hands, destroyed the image, became a great mountain, and filled the whole earth.

Daniel informed the king that the four sections of the image were four successive kingdoms, the first one being his own Babylonian empire (2:38). The interpretation concluded:

> And whereas thou sawest iron mixed with miry clay, they shall mingle themselves with the seed of men; but they shall not cleave one to another, even as iron is not mixed with clay. And in the days of these kings shall the God of heaven set up a kingdom, which shall never be destroyed, and the kingdom shall not be left to another people, but it shall break in pieces and consume all these kingdoms, and it shall stand for ever (2:43-44).

Daniel 7 is the account of the dream of Daniel. He saw four beasts or creatures. The description of the fourth beast is:

> After this I saw in the night visions, and behold a fourth beast, dreadful and terrible, and strong exceedingly; and it had great iron teeth: it devoured and brake in pieces, and stamped the residue with the feet of it: and it was diverse from all the beasts that were before it; and it had ten horns (7:7).

After the fourth beast appears, then the "saints of the most High shall take the kingdom, and possess the kingdom for ever, even for ever and ever" (7:18). The

113

two aspects of the dream of the prophet that distinguish it from the dream of the king are the "little horn" that grows up from among the ten horns, and the ten horns themselves. It is only assumed that the image had ten toes. The four empires seen in the four parts of the image and the four beasts are commonly accepted to be (a) Babylonian under Nebuchadnezzar, (b) Medo-Persian under Darius and Cyrus, (c) Greco-Macedonian of Alexander the Great, and (d) Roman Empire of the Caesars.[6] Four earthly empires will appear on the stage of world history. No more, just four, and then the eternal kingdom will be established. The dreams do not affirm that no other earthly empires will appear after the eternal kingdom is established. The principal element of the prophetic visions is *time*. "In the days of these kings—that is, the rulers of the fourth empire—is the time set for the establishment of the kingdom of God (2:44).

There are two standard interpretations of the "little horn." The one sees fulfillment in the church. It identifies the "little horn" with the "man of sin" (II Thess. 2:3), the last of the antichrists. Many have applied it directly to the papacy. The dispensational view is of the "little horn" as the future king of the restored Roman Empire who is to be revealed at the rapture of the church. This interpretation means that the prophecy skips over the church completely.

Whatever the exact application of the "little horn,"

6 Not considered a live option is the liberal view that divides the Medo-Persian Empire, attributing the Median Empire to the silver/bear beast kingdom and the Persian to the brazen/leopard kingdom. This view makes the ten horns the successors of Alexander the Great and the "little horn" Antiochus Epiphanes. The purpose of this division is to remove the element of supernatural prophecy, placing the authorship of Daniel in the Seleucid period. This makes the "little horn" a veiled attack upon Antiochus (175-164 B.C.) by an unknown author who projects his material back to the exilic period.

the prophecy of the kingdom points to the church. The most reasonable interpretation of the two visions taken together is that in the days of the fourth (Roman) empire the eternal kingdom appears. This sees the ten horns on the fourth beast as ten tributary kings and kingdoms.

One of the pivotal aspects of the Daniel 7 prophecy is the identification of the "saints of the most High" who "take the kingdom, and possess the kingdom for ever." Either these are Christians or they are Jewish saints. The difficulty dispensationalists have with the parenthesis theory is that the system forbids it being church saints. The standard dispensational arrangement of the prophetic schedule has the church raptured and absent at the time of the beginning of the activity of Christ on the earth. Oswald T. Allis points out that the first edition of the *Scofield Bible* said that the saints of Daniel 7 are church saints.[7] The dispensational school regards the doctrine that the church saints will reign with Christ as clearly taught in the New Testament. But this so neatly contradicted the church parenthesis theory, that the revised edition changed the comment to read: "That church saints will also share in the rule seems clear from Acts 16:17; Romans 8:17; II Timothy 2:10-12; I Peter 2:9; Revelation 1:6; 3:21." Thus, the system which gnashes its teeth at the thought of Christ ruling in corporeal absentia, finds itself affirming that, for a time, the church saints will be doing exactly that.

Concerning the time of the kingdom, it is a study in itself how dispensationalism has conveniently imported a "gap" between the sixty-ninth and the seventieth week of Daniel 9. It is explained that the "timeclock stops." The only justification for this gap is the necessity of preserving the system of Biblical interpretation. The content of Daniel 9 is obviously a *time* prophecy. Of

[7] *Prophecy and the Church* (Philadelphia: The Presbyterian and Reformed Pub. Co., 1945), p. 127.

what use is the "clock" of Daniel if it stops? The gap destroys the essential content, nature, and purpose of the prophecy.

Armstrong's affirmation that the prophecies of Daniel were closed until the latter half of the twentieth century is simply another verse of this same song.

Of the many positions Armstrong is forced to defend is the logical necessity of having a restoration of the Roman Empire. The prophetic picture was clear that the kingdom would come at the time of the fourth empire. The fourth empire came and went, and the kind of kingdom both first-century Jews and twentieth-century dispensationalists had decided upon failed to appear. The church is brushed aside as a contingency. Therefore, the fourth empire must be again made available so Israel can be restored. Armstrongites explain:

> Let's speak plainly: the prophecies of your Bible reveal that in this end-time there would be the seventh and final revival (or resurrection) of the Roman Empire.[8]

How strange it is to hear those accusing their opponents of "spiritualizing away the Scriptures" affirm that nearly every European government since the fall of Rome is the Roman Empire. Sad that "Eternal Rome" has not been so eternal as the old Jewish error. A man who looks at modern Europe and sees the Roman Empire ought have no difficulty in looking at the church and seeing the kingdom.

The time prophecies of Daniel lead a reader to expect the kingdom in the days of the Roman Empire. How comfortable, then, is the plain statement of Jesus in Galilee—while the Caesars ruled in Rome—that the time had arrived for the kingdom:

> Now after that John was put in prison, Jesus

8 Raymond F. McNair, "A Strong United Europe," *Tomorrow's World,* February, 1970, p. 33.

came into Galilee, preaching the gospel of the
kingdom of God, And saying, The time is fulfilled, and the kingdom of God is at hand: repent
ye, and believe the gospel (Mark 1:14-15).

"The time is fulfilled." That was almost two thousand years ago. Only a stern prejudice in favor of a
particular system of prophetic theology could cause one
to miss this. Jesus promised on the borders of Caesarea
Philippi to build His church, to give to Peter the keys to
the kingdom, and said that some standing there would
not die until they saw the Son of man coming in His
kingdom (Matt. 16:18-28). The rule of Christ after the
resurrection was complete, for all authority had been
given unto Him (Matt. 28:18). He began to rule on the
throne of David and the church was established as His
kingdom (Acts 2:30-33). He has taken His place on the
"right hand of the Majesty on high" (Heb. 1:3). The
writer to the Hebrews rejoices that the kingdom is now
here, and that we have received it (12:28). Those who
have obeyed the gospel have been "translated . . . into
the kingdom of his dear Son" (Col. 1:13). At the coming
of Christ the kingdom will not be established but will be
delivered up to the Father:

> But every man in his own order: Christ the
> firstfruits; afterward they that are Christ's at his
> coming. Then cometh the end, when he shall
> have delivered up the kingdom to God, even the
> Father; when he shall have put down all rule and
> all authority and power. For he must reign, till
> he hath put all enemies under his feet. The last
> enemy that shall be destroyed is death (I Cor.
> 15:23-26).

To push the establishment of the kingdom to the
Second Coming of Jesus does violence to this text. It
puts a thousand years or more between His coming and
the "then." The word *eita*, "then," normally means
"that which follows immediately." If a millennial reign
were to be understood as inserted here, the proper word

would be "later." Dispensationalism affirms that Jesus is not really reigning now, which is strange if He really has "all authority." Nothing is more than "all." It denies that death is destroyed with the resurrection of the dead. The passage says that when death is destroyed, the kingdom rule of the Son will be ended and He will deliver the kingdom to the Father. The order in Scripture is: (a) the reign, and (b) the destruction of death. The dispensational order is: (a) the resurrection of the redeemed dead, (b) the translation of the redeemed living, and (c) the establishment of the reign.

Prophecy and the church. If the church is not the promised kingdom, then it follows that the large body of Old Testament prophecy does not deal with the church, but remains for the return of Jesus to find fulfillment. All brands of dispensationalism concede this point. One writer says, "Thus the Church came in as a mystery, and was but rarely, if at all, spoken of in the Old Testament prophecies."[9] Armstrong says that "Few realize that the prophecies of the Old Testament pertain, primarily, to this 20th century."[10]

It is preposterous to push the hope of Israel to the future. In the earliest days of the church, Peter preached:

> Yea, and all the prophets from Samuel and those that follow after, as many as have spoken, have likewise foretold of *these* days (Acts 3:24).

(If the prophecies of Daniel were closed "until the latter half of the twentieth century," then Peter was wrong.) Paul viewed the preaching of the death and resurrection of Jesus as the culmination of the prophetic message of the Old Testament:

> Having therefore obtained help of God, I

9 W. E. B., *Jesus Is Coming* (New York and London: Fleming H. Revell Co., 1932), p. 89.

10 *USBCP*, p. 132.

continue unto this day, witnessing both to small and great, saying none other things than those which the prophets and Moses did say should come: That Christ should suffer, and that he should be the first that should rise from the dead, and should shew light unto the people, and to the Gentiles (Acts 26:22-23).

A recurring theme in Acts is the practice of the apostles to preach the message of Christ "from the Scriptures." If it is true that the church is rarely, if at all, mentioned in the Old Testament, then they must have preached on little else than the Second Coming.

The kingdom not of the world. Jesus said, "My kingdom is not of this world" (John 18:36). Both Armstrong and all other kinds of dispensationalism insist that it is. The Jews thought it must certainly be earthly and temporal. Jesus was plainly assuring Pilate that Rome need not fear for the throne of the emperor, because His kingdom was not that kind of kingdom. Armstrong says, in effect, "Of course it is that kind of kingdom. It is precisely that kind of kingdom." Jesus taught unmistakably that He would rule over His kingdom in corporeal absentia:

> And as they heard these things, he added and spake a parable, because he was nigh to Jerusalem, and because they thought that the kingdom of God should immediately appear. He said therefore, A certain nobleman went into a far country to receive for himself a kingdom, and to return. And he called his ten servants, and delivered them ten pounds, and said unto them, Occupy till I come (Luke 19:11-13).

The context is that the Jews expected the Messiah to begin the necessary divine revolution and set up the Throne of David. Since Jesus was nearing Jerusalem, the time must be ripe. So He tells them this parable to teach them the truth. The essential elements of the parable are these: (*a*) He was going into a "far country," not staying in Jerusalem, and receive a kingdom; (*b*) He would

119

receive a kingdom *there;* and (*c*) upon His return His servants would be rewarded and His enemies destroyed. This parable is unfortunate for the dispensational school of thought, for the order is all wrong. Dispensationalism corrects it to proceed: (*a*) the return, (*b*) the receiving of the kingdom, (*c*) the thousand-year reign, and (*d*) judgment.

In perfect harmony with this parable is the kingdom prophecy of Daniel 7:

> And I saw in the night visions, and, behold, one like the Son of man came with the clouds of heaven, and came to the Ancient of days, and they brought him near before him. And there was given him dominion, and glory, and a kingdom, that all people, nations, and languages, should serve him: his dominion is an everlasting dominion, which shall not pass away, and his kingdom that which shall not be destroyed (vv. 13-14).

The Son of man came to the "Ancient of days"—that is, God—not to earth, and received His kingdom. He came with the clouds of heaven. Luke records, "And when he had spoken these things, while they beheld, he was taken up; and a cloud received him out of their sight" (Acts 1:9). He ascends to God "in a far country" and receives His kingdom, and later will return to judge.

Millennium

No survey of the subject of prophecy can ignore Revelation 20:1-6. This section is not an exegesis of the text, but a list of observations.

The "thousand years" section of Revelation 20 is the source of the term "millennium." It is the only source. The "thousand years" appears nowhere else. It is the dispensational claim that this chapter teaches: (*a*) the second coming of Christ, (*b*) the bodily resurrection of the saints, (*c*) the reign of Christ on the earth, and (*d*) the throne in Jerusalem. It is strange that this chapter teaches all these things when it mentions not one of them. The only reign mentioned is that of the spirits of martyred saints "with Christ."

Twenty figures of speech appear in chapters 19 and 20 of Revelation alone. The dispensational preacher understands all or nearly all the twenty figures in a symbolic way. He then looks up from his Bible and without even blinking asserts that the "thousand years" means literally that because "that's what the Bible says, doesn't it?"

The Last Days

Among the prophetic elements pushed forward to the return of Jesus and the supposed beginning of a millennial reign over the nations on earth is the principle of the "last days." If the church is a mere contingency, then room must be made for God at last to work things out—that is, the kingdom. And if the general dispensational scheme is accurate, then the "church age" cannot be the last days. But the New Testament testifies that the days of the church are indeed the prophetic last days. If inspired New Testament speakers or writers point to Old Testament last-days prophecies and then point to events with a "this is that," then no basis remains for pushing other uses of last days to the end of the time of the church, or to a millennium. Last means last. A thing is either the last of a series, or it is not last. If the days of the church are next-to-last, how foolish of the prophets to call them last. It is difficult to conceive of a thousand-year period as being so incidental in the prophetic schedule of God that it could be inserted after the dispensation of the last days.

Peter at Pentecost defended himself and the others against the charge of drunkenness by pointing to Joel 2:28-32 and claiming fulfillment:

121

> For these are not drunken, as ye suppose, seeing it is but the third hour of the day. But *this is that* which was spoken by the prophet Joel; And it shall come to pass *in the last days*, saith God, I will pour out of my Spirit upon all flesh: and your sons and your daughters shall prophesy, and your young men shall see visions, and your old men shall dream dreams (Acts 2:15-17).

The writer to the Hebrew Christians affirms that "these" days are last days. He begins the Hebrew epistle:

> God, who at sundry times and in divers manners spake in time past unto the fathers by the prophets, Hath in these *last days* spoken unto us by his Son, whom he hath appointed heir of all things, by whom also he made the worlds (1:1-2).

The main avenue of communication between God and man had been the prophets. Now this has been replaced by the Son who is seated at the "right hand of the Majesty on high" (1:3). The teaching in this text is that attention is focused away from the prophets and onto the atoning and mediatorial work of the Son. This is to be expected if the death, burial, and resurrection of Jesus are the culmination and fulfillment of the message of Moses and the prophets, and not just an unfortunate interruption in the original plan of God to restore Israel.

If the "these days" of the church is not the last days or end days of the prophetic schedule, then in what sense were the day of Pentecost and subsequent years the last days of anything? Those were the *first* days of the church, now almost two thousand years old.

Paul warned Timothy of the troubles that would characterize the last days (II Tim. 3:1 ff.). No principle of interpretation enunciated in Scripture allows the term to mean one thing in the preaching of Peter in quoting Joel and another thing in this warning. The difficulty described began in the days of the ministry of Timothy.

122

The heresy and sin are placed in contrast to the soundness and fidelity of the young preacher (3:10).

Peter says that the last days will be the time of the scoffer and the lustful and the unbeliever (II Peter 3:3). The unbelief described did not wait until this generation to appear. Heresy, blasphemy, scoffing, and lust are the antithesis of conditions posited by the dispensationalist for the temporal reign of Jesus in what he considers to be the last days.

John affirms that the days of the church are to be thought of as final:

> Little children, it is the last time [hour]: and as ye have heard that antichrist shall come, even now are there many antichrists; whereby we know that it is the last time (I John 2:18).

The dispensational principle that last days for the church is one thing and last days for Israel is another cannot hold here. The clear meaning of the apostle was that his contemporaries shared with him the sometimes doubtful privilege of being in the last time. It cannot be a national reign of Jesus in victory because antichrist is undefeated. It cannot be the end of the period of the church, because it was written in the beginning *about* the beginning.

If these days are the last days, then it is expected that "Samuel and those that follow after, as many as have spoken, have likewise foretold of these days" (Acts 3:24). What did Samuel say about the death and resurrection of Jesus and the beginning of the church? *Literally*, nothing! Armstrong and his dispensational bedfellows who vociferously equate literalism in understanding prophecy with orthodoxy, are faced with the fact that most of the prophets did not literally speak of the things about which Peter was preaching and of the things that happened in the first century as "these days." What did Samuel and those that followed after—

"as many as have spoken"—promise? They promised kingdom restoration, new covenant, and spiritual blessing. If Peter was right in saying that Samuel spoke of "these days," then the kingdom must have been going on in "these days," because the kingdom and the throne of David is what Samuel wrote about. If the throne of David had been postponed to future last days, then Samuel was as silent as the tomb about the early days of the church.

Jesus unmistakably taught that the main body of prophecy was focused upon His death, His resurrection, and the preaching of the gospel. In His appearance to the eleven after the resurrection He taught them how to view all of the Old Testament:

> And he said unto them, These are the words which I spake unto you, while I was yet with you, that all things must be fulfilled, which were written in the law of Moses, and in the prophets, and in the psalms, concerning me. Then opened he their understanding, that they might understand the scriptures, And said unto them, Thus it is written, and thus it behoved Christ to suffer, and to rise from the dead the third day: And that repentance and remission of sins should be preached in his name among all nations, beginning at Jerusalem (Luke 24:44-47).

This text is decisive. The apostles did not understand the Old Testament, even after being under the Master Teacher for three years. The Jews thought the Messiah was going to establish a temporal kingdom with an earthly throne, and they rejected and condemned Him for not doing so. They were wrong. Armstrong understands the Old Testament the same way. He is wrong. All that was written by Moses, the prophets, and in the Psalms was the subject of the lesson taught by Jesus that day. The Second Coming was not mentioned. He taught about His death and resurrection and the beginning of the church in Jerusalem. From Moses, the prophets, and the Psalms, dispensationalists teach about

124

little else than the Second Coming. Where in the Old Testament is it "written" that "repentance and remission of sins should be preached in his name among all nations, beginning at Jerusalem"? *Literally*, nowhere! The duplicate prophecies of Micah 4:1-7 and Isaiah 2:1-5 are the only Old Testament Scriptures that speak of the word of the Lord going out from Jerusalem. When an Armstrongite or confirmed dispensationalist drops his Bible, it falls open to Isaiah 2:

> And it shall come to pass in the last days, that the mountain of the LORD'S house shall be established in the top of the mountains, and shall be exalted above the hills; and all nations shall flow unto it. And many people shall go and say, Come ye, and let us go up to the mountain of the LORD, to the house of the God of Jacob; and he will teach us of his ways, and we will walk in his paths: for out of Zion shall go forth the law, *and the word of the LORD from Jerusalem.* And he shall judge among the nations, and shall rebuke many people: and they shall beat their swords into plowshares, and their spears into pruning-hooks: nation shall not lift up sword against nation, neither shall they learn war any more (vv. 2-4).

Jesus "opened their understanding that they might understand" that "thus it is written" in this last days prophecy that "repentance and remission of sins should be preached in his name among all nations, beginning at Jerusalem." They were to witness the fulfillment (Luke 24:48). The peaceful conditions of Isaiah 2:2-4 were to be brought about by the church, within which men of all nations have peace one with another. To cite Isaiah 2 as a picture of the "wonderful world of tomorrow" is to deny what Jesus taught about it.

Spiritual Promises

The spiritual promise to Abraham that "in thee shall all families of the earth be blessed" (Gen. 12:3) has been fulfilled in Christ. The promise is not anticipating a future dispensation for fulfillment:

> And the scripture, foreseeing that God would justify the heathen [Gentiles] through faith, preached before the gospel unto Abraham, saying, In thee shall all nations be blessed. So then they which be of faith are blessed with faithful Abraham (Gal. 3:8-9).

> And if ye be Christ's, then are ye Abraham's seed, and heirs according to the promise (Gal. 3:29).

Jeremiah gave the spiritual promise to Israel:

> But this shall be the covenant that I will make with the house of Israel; After those days, saith the LORD, I will put my law in their inward parts, and write it in their hearts; and will be their God, and they shall be my people (31:33).

The New Testament makes it clear when and how this covenant arrived:

> But this man, after he had offered one sacrifice for sins for ever, sat down on the right hand of God; From henceforth expecting till his enemies be made his footstool [Psalm 110:1]. For by one offering he hath perfected for ever them that are sanctified. Whereof the Holy Ghost also is a witness to us: for after that he had said before, This is the covenant that I will make with them after those days, saith the Lord, I will put my laws into their hearts, and in their minds will I write them; And their sins and iniquities will I remember no more (Heb. 10:12-17).

Not only is the new covenant of Jeremiah 31 spoken of as fulfilled in the death, resurrection, and ascension of Jesus, but also Psalm 110 cited as prophetic proof of the same. This key "kingdom" psalm is used by dispensationalists as a proof text. Dispensationalists may affirm that the psalm looks to the time when Christ will appear, but Paul states that it looks to the time when He ascended; and he connects it undeniably with the present reign of Christ "on the right hand of God."

The "one offering" of Jesus was sufficient to meet the spiritual requirements of the new covenant. Jesus said, "This is the new testament [covenant] in my blood" (I Cor. 11:25). Shall there be another covenant with more spiritual promises? If so, then the spiritual promises claimed by the church are incomplete. Paul wrote that "if that first covenant had been faultless, then should no place have been sought for the second." It follows, then, that if the second covenant is perfect, no place will be needed for a third. The affirmation that the spiritual promises require a temporal "rod of iron" rule of Christ upon earth is a denial of the adequacy of the blood of Jesus and the gift of the Holy Spirit. The new covenant has the potential to bring a man to "the stature of the fulness of Christ" (Eph. 4:13). To desire a move from the new covenant in the blood of Jesus to a restoration of Temple worship and the Jewish theocracy, is to desire a move from riches to rags.

Summary and Conclusions

The Bible is clear. The hope of Israel is a promise kept and a prophecy fulfilled. If Israel did exist as a political or ethnic entity today, she could present God with no promissory note yet unpaid. Israel received her land. Israel received her restoration. Israel has had the opportunity to be "born again" into the kingdom and to be ruled by Christ on the Davidic throne, and she still has that opportunity. Israel potentially is, with the Gentiles, "Abraham's seed, and heirs according to the promise" in Christ. If the "Ten Lost Tribes of Israel" appear today with genealogical record intact, or if the Jews rebuild the Temple in Jerusalem and resume Mosaic worship, it will have no prophetic significance as far as the plan of salvation is concerned:

127

For he is our peace, who hath made both one, and hath broken down the middle wall of partition between us; Having abolished in his flesh the enmity, even the law of commandments contained in ordinances; for to make in himself of twain one new man, so making peace; And that he might reconcile both unto God in one body by the cross, having slain the enmity thereby (Eph. 2:14-16).

The hope of Israel is to be reconciled to God by the cross. Israel has no other hope.

5 THE SABBATH AND THE LAW

Armstrong moves from the Jewish error of the kingdom to the Jewish error of the Sabbath and the Law. He sees the Sabbath as the independent and eternal covenant that identifies the people of God. Armstrong sets up the standard Seventh-Day Adventist dichotomy of moral law versus ceremonial or ritualistic law. The Sabbath is a part of the Ten Commandments or moral law. This has never been abrogated. (He affirms that the ceremonial law will be reinstituted in the coming kingdom.) He sees salvation being yet future in the "God family," which salvation is accomplished ultimately through character growth in obedience to the "government of God" and not through the cross. The following is the basic material which demonstrates the error of the Armstrongite doctrine of Sabbath and Law:

1. The Sabbath "forever." The basic argument offered by Armstrong for an eternal Sabbath is from the word "forever" (Exod. 31:16, 17). He argues that since "forever" is still going on, the Sabbath commandment is still binding.

The fact is that the Hebrew word *olam*, "forever," has as its root meaning "a long, indefinite period of time." It usually does *not* mean eternal or without end. Often it is used of the past as in Genesis 6:4, "mighty men . . . of *old*." The reader is urged to secure an analytical concordance or lexicon and check for himself. The idea of eternity is conveyed in the Hebrew language by

129

comparison and deduction, rather than in express words.

In arguing for an independent and eternal covenant, Armstrong would be in a more defensible position if he had selected the covenant of circumcision. Perhaps he would have if Paul had not so explicitly stated that if a man submitted to circumcision as a requirement for salvation he becomes debtor to do the whole law and is fallen from grace (Gal. 5:1-4). It is also stated that circumcision was to be an "everlasting" (*olam*) covenant (Gen. 17:13). The fact is that the Sabbath was an *olam* covenant in the same way that circumcision was an *olam* covenant. And as for being a covenant independent of the ceremonial law, circumcision would be the logical nominee. Circumcision was instituted with Abraham, whereas the Sabbath was not observed until Moses (Exod. 16:23).

2. Traditional Christianity observes nine of the Ten Commandments or moral laws. The Worldwide Church of God observes all ten. Such is the defense of misled Armstrongites. Armstrongite logic affirms that if a man does not steal, kill, or commit adultery, he is thereby obeying the Mosaic moral code. Conversely, if he is not under the moral law, he is free to practice the things therein prohibited. What a lot of foolishness!

The Ten Commandments did not make honesty, reverence, and purity moral attributes. They were right long before Sinai. The principles of the Decalogue appeared in that code because they expressed the will of God. Those principles were not right because they were engraved on the tablets of stone.

A Christian is moral because he is in Christ, not because he is under the Law. Armstrongite logic would affirm that because the American Revolution removed the colonies from the rule of British law, the fathers of our country were therefore free to do anything that was formerly prohibited. There was a British law against murder. The men who autographed the Declaration of Independence were therefore declaring themselves free to kill. The obvious truth is that they were simply declaring themselves to be under a different law.

The Gentile world was never free from the obligations of righteousness just because it was not party to the Sinaitic covenant (Rom. 2).

3. Moral law versus ceremonial law. Nowhere does the Bible make such a distinction. To understand the folly of this dichotomy, simply listen to the teachings of Jesus concerning the "greatest commandment."

In Matthew 22 the record is that a lawyer asked Jesus,

> Which is the great commandment in the law? Jesus said unto him, Thou shalt love the Lord thy God with all thy heart, and with all thy soul, and with all thy mind. This is the first and great commandment. And the second is like unto it, Thou shalt love thy neighbour as thyself. On these two commandments hang all the law and the prophets (vv. 36-40).

These two commandments, on which are suspended all the law and the prophets, are not in the Decalogue at all. They are part of the "ritualistic law" (see Deut. 6:5; Lev. 19:18). Are we to believe that the "moral law" has been continued whereas the law which is the "great" commandment and which is foundational to that moral law is abrogated?

4. The Ten Commandments, the way to salvation? If the doctrine that the Decalogue is binding today cannot stand, Armstrongism comes apart at the seams. Armstrongism is a system of law. The gospel is a system of grace. "For the law was given by Moses, but grace and truth came by Jesus Christ" (John 1:17).

Scripture is so plain on this that one will have to have professional help to miss it:

> Such is the confidence that we have through Christ toward God. Not that we are sufficient of ourselves to claim anything as coming from us; our sufficiency is from God, who has qualified us

131

to be ministers of a new covenant, *not in a written code* but in the Spirit; *for the written code kills*, but the Spirit gives life. Now if the *dispensation of death, carved in letters on stone*, came with such splendor that the Israelites could not look at Moses' face because of its brightness, fading as this was, will not the dispensation of the Spirit be attended with greater splendor? For if there was splendor in the *dispensation of condemnation*, the dispensation of righteousness must far exceed it in splendor. Indeed, in this case, what once had splendor has come to have no splendor at all, because of the splendor that surpasses it. For if what *faded away* came with splendor, *what is permanent* must have much more splendor. Since we have such a hope, we are very bold, not like Moses, who put a veil over his face so that the Israelites might not see the end of the fading splendor. But their minds were hardened; for to this day, when they read the old covenant, that same veil remains unlifted, because only through Christ is it taken away (II Cor. 3:4-14, RSV).

There it is. The written code that kills and has faded away was the one carved in letters on stone and delivered by Moses as he had the veil over his face (Exod. 34:29-35). The Ten Commandments inform and condemn of sin, but forgiveness is in Christ. Armstrong is preaching the "dispensation of condemnation." All who follow him will find at the Judgment that the Ten Commandments are the indictment that will prove them guilty before God, and they will have no Savior.

5. Was the Sabbath nailed to the cross? Armstrongism goes far beyond Adventism in binding the Sabbath upon men. II Corinthians 3 affirms that the Ten Commandments were abolished as a binding code. The Sabbath is one of the ten. How logical it is then to read further on the subject in the Epistle to the Colossians:

And you, who were dead in trespasses and the uncircumcision of your flesh, God made alive together with him, having forgiven us all our

132

> trespasses, having canceled the bond which stood
> against us with its legal demands; this he set
> aside, nailing it to the cross. He disarmed the
> principalities and powers and made a public
> example of them, triumphing over them in him.
> Therefore let no one pass judgment on you in
> questions of food and drink or with regard to a
> festival or a new moon or *a sabbath*. These are
> only a shadow of what is to come; but the
> substance belongs to Christ (2:13-17, RSV).

The Law made us guilty (Rom. 3:19). But God has "forgiven us all our trespasses." He "canceled the bond" with its legal demands and nailed it to the cross. He openly demonstrated that man was free from the condemnation of the Law through Christ. Therefore men were not to permit themselves to be judged in regard to the requirements of the Law, including the Sabbath.[1] God has made a public example of man's inability to keep the Law, and He made manifest at the cross the way of salvation. No one need miss it. Pity that Armstrong didn't get the message. He wrests the canceled bond from the cross. He declares man's continuing responsibility to obey it. He makes binding Mosaic legal requirements, including the Sabbath. He is living in the "shadow" (Col. 2:17). It is the shadow of death. All who believe in Armstrong enough to allow him to convince them that Paul is wrong here, are living in the shadow of death. Armstrong stands with the mocking crowd at the foot of the cross. He understands no better than they what happened at Calvary.

[1] It is argued by Sabbatarians that the plural word for Sabbath (sabbatōn) of Colossians 2:16 means Sabbath observances other than the Sabbath Day. The word Sabbath was commonly written in the plural, even when referring to a specific Sabbath Day. In fact the form (genitive plural) found in Colossians 2:16 is also found in Acts 13:14 and 16:13 where it refers to a particular Sabbath Day.

6. Was the Sabbath a part of the Old Covenant? Hear Armstrong:

> I have said that God made the Sabbath a SEPARATE, ETERNAL, and PERPETUAL COVENANT, entirely separate and apart from what we term the Old Covenant made at Mt. Sinai.[2]

Now hear the writer to the Hebrews:

> But now hath he obtained a more excellent ministry, by how much also he is the mediator of a better covenant, which was established upon better promises. For if that first covenant had been faultless, then should no place have been sought for the second. For finding fault with them, he saith, Behold, the days come, saith the Lord, when I will make a new covenant with the house of Israel and with the house of Judah: Not according to the covenant that I made with their fathers in the day when I took them by the hand to lead them out of the land of Egypt; because they continued not in my covenant, and I regarded them not, saith the Lord. For this is the covenant that I will make with the house of Israel after those days, saith the Lord; I will put my laws into their mind, and write them in their hearts: and I will be to them a God, and they shall be to me a people (8:6-10).

The citation by the writer here is Jeremiah 31:31. The covenant was made with Israel when God "took them by the hand to lead them out of the land of Egypt."

> There was nothing in the ark save the two tables of stone, which Moses put there at Horeb, when the LORD made a covenant with the children of Israel, when they came out of the land of Egypt (I Kings 8:9).
> And I have set there a place for the ark, wherein is the covenant of the LORD, which he

2 USBCP, p. 161.

made with our fathers, when he brought them
out of the land of Egypt (I Kings 8:21).

Only Armstrong speaks of *two* covenants being made
with Israel when God brought them out of Egypt. The
Bible speaks of one. There was nothing in the ark but
the tables of stone in the time of Solomon. In the ark
was the covenant God made with Israel at the Exodus.
Therefore that covenant was the Ten Commandments.

7. The Sabbath and the Lord's Day. The Sabbath
was a part of the covenant made with Israel only. They
were to use it to remember that God had delivered them
from Egyptian bondage (Deut. 5:15). The first day of
the week is the new Lord's day.

Jesus rose from the dead on the first day of the
week. Armstrong argues for a Wednesday crucifixion and
a Sabbath resurrection. The purpose is to remove the
significance of the first day, thereby to bolster Sabba-
tarianism. The New Testament does not explicitly state
that the church kept the first day *because* this was the
day of the resurrection. And it does not necessarily
follow that a Saturday resurrection would nullify first-
day observance. But the evidence is clear that the resurrection was on the first day of the week, and it is a
reasonable inference to link the day with Lord's Day
keeping.

Armstrongite doctrine of Wednesday crucifixion is
built upon Matthew 12:40: "For as Jonas was three days
and three nights in the whale's belly; so shall the Son of
man be three days and three nights in the heart of the
earth." The argument is that the "only proof"[3] of the
claims of the Lord to be Messiah is a seventy-two-hour
sojourn in the tomb.

The pivotal aspect of the "sign of Jonas" is not the
duration of the occupation of Joseph's tomb, but the
resurrection itself. And it is typical Armstrongite Biblical

---

[3] Herman L. Hoeh, *The Crucifixion Was Not on Friday!* (Pasadena: Radio Church of God), p. 1.

135

interpretation to jump up and down on one verse to the studied exclusion of all other texts pertaining to the subject at hand. Purely on the basis of the words "three days and three nights," Armstrongite doctrine is that Jesus was to rise:

> ... Not even in two and one-half days, but IN THREE DAYS' TIME—72 hours. In other words, in exactly three days and three nights, at the precise moment, three 24-hour days after his death and burial.[4]

The Scriptures will not permit such an arbitrary exploitation of a particular phraseology. In Mark 8:31 it is "after three days"; Matthew 16:21, "the third day"; Matthew 17:23, "the third day"; Matthew 20:19, "and the third day he shall rise again"; Luke 9:22, "and be raised the third day." When all concerned material is surveyed, it is found that a part of a day is spoken of as a day. To insist that "three days" must mean exactly seventy-two hours is a study in foolishness. When we say "three days ago" we seldom mean exactly seventy-two hours past. Men have never been that precise in the use of this terminology. They were not in the first century. They are not now. Armstrong insists that the seventy-two-hour requirement thrusts the crucifixion back to Wednesday and makes the resurrection seventy-two hours later—that is, on the Sabbath.

The question is settled by the two disciples on the road to Emmaus. Luke 24:1 begins, "Now upon the first day of the week." The action moves from the empty sepulchre to the conversation between two disciples as they walked toward Emmaus "that same day" (24:13). They relate the events of the past few days to the incognito Master. They speak of the crucifixion (24:20) and establish an accurate chronology by explaining that "to-day is the third day since these things were done" (24:21). There it is. If the crucifixion had been Wednes-

4 *Ibid.*

day, then the first day of the week could not have been the third day since the crucifixion.

Armstrongites argue that "Monday, not Sunday, was the third day from Friday."[5] They have lost the argument. If Monday must be the third day from Friday, then Sunday must be the third day from Thursday. The best Armstrongites can get from Luke 24 is a Thursday crucifixion.

In order to hold for a Wednesday crucifixion, Armstrong argues that the year of the crucifixion had to be A.D. 31, thus making the crucifixion on April 25. (The passover was slain the day following the first new moon after the spring equinox.) But the astronomic possibilities for a Friday date for the cross are: A.D. 27, Friday, April 11; A.D. 29, Friday, March 18; A.D. 30, Friday, April 7; A.D. 33, Friday, April 3.

The apostolic church met for worship on the first day of the week: Acts 20:7; 2:42; I Corinthians 16:1-2. It is called the Lord's Day, not the Sabbath (Rev. 1:10). Sabbatarians argue that because Paul preached in the synagogue every Sabbath, he was observing the day as the Lord's Day. As a matter of fact, he did not enter the synagogue every Sabbath. For example, when he came to Ephesus he began going to the synagogue every Sabbath to preach (not to worship). This lasted for three months (Acts 19:8). Then they rejected him and for the next two years he held sessions in the school of Tyrannus. And if Paul's entrance into the synagogue for preaching was the church at worship, then what was his ministry to the pagan citadel, the Areopagus (Acts 17)? If his presence in the synagogue on the Sabbath constituted Christian worship, then his presence among the heathen statuary of Athens for the same purpose (preaching) must logically be Christian worship.

Jesus rose from the dead on the first day of the week. He repeatedly met with His disciples on the first

5 *Ibid.*, p. 2.

day of the week, following the resurrection (John 20:1, 19, 26). Pentecost came on the first day of the week (Lev. 23:15). The Holy Spirit overwhelmed the apostles on the first day of the week. The church assembled to break bread and gather offerings on the first day of the week. The old covenant had a special day set aside in it, the Sabbath. How fitting that the new covenant (Heb. 8:13) should have a new day!

The apostolic and early Christian fathers unanimously affirm first-day observance:

Epistle of Barnabas, ca. A.D. 120:
> Wherefore, also, we keep on the eighth day with joyfulness, the day, also, on which Jesus rose again from the dead.

Didache, ca. A.D. 80-120.
> But every Lord's Day do ye gather your selves together to break bread, and give thanksgiving. . . .

Justin Martyr, A.D. 140:
> And on the day called Sunday, all who live in cities or in the country gather together to one place, and the memoirs of the apostles or the writings of the prophets are read, as long as time permits; then, when the reader has ceased, the president verbally instructs and exhorts to the imitation of these good things. Then we all rise together and pray, and, as we before said, when our prayer is ended, bread and wine and water are brought, and the president in like manner offers prayers and thanksgivings. . . .

> But Sunday is the day on which we all hold our common assembly, because it is the first day on which God, having wrought a change in the darkness and matter, made the world; and Jesus Christ, our Savior, on the same day rose from the dead. He was crucified on the day before that of Saturn (Saturday); and on the day after that of Saturn, which is the day of the sun, having appeared to His apostles and disciples, He taught them these things, which we have submitted to you also for your consideration.

Bardasanes of Edessa, Syria, A.D. 180:

> For, lo, wherever we be, all of us are called by the one name of the Messiah, Christians, and upon one day, which is the first day of the week, we assemble ourselves together.

Tertullian of Africa, A.D. 200:

> We solemnize the day after Saturday. . . .

Origen, A.D. 225:

> But if it be clear from the Holy Scriptures that God rained manna from Heaven on the Lord's Day, and rained none on the Sabbath Day, let the Jews understand that from that time our Lord's Day was set above the true Sabbath. . . .

Cyprian, Bishop of Carthage, A.D. 253:

> Because the eighth day, that is the first day after the Sabbath, was to be that on which the Lord should rise again, and should quicken us . . . the eighth day, that is, the first day after the Sabbath, and the Lord's Day. . . .

Eusebius, A.D. 324 (speaking of some Judaizers of his time):

> With them the observance of the law was altogether necessary. . . . They also observe the sabbath and other disciplines of the Jews just like them, but on the other hand they also celebrate the Lord's Day very much like us in the commemoration of his resurrection.

Armstrong makes much of the proposition that Sunday was a pagan Roman religious day, and that the apostate church appropriated it. Not so.

The pagan Romans and Greeks did not have a regular weekly day of rest and worship. Nor did they have a weekly festival or assembly in behalf of the gods. There was no special day of the week when they went to the temples to pray and make offerings. For both Romans and Greeks, the month was the unit, not the week. The month was generally divided into three periods of ten days: the Kalend, first; the Nones, fifth or seventh; and the Ides, thirteenth or fifteenth. These divisions had no religious significance. In the Roman calendar were "nun-dial" or market days. These came at periods of eight or nine days. It was, in a sense, a regular stoppage of work, but it had no religious overtones. The sun was not worshiped on Sunday, the moon was not worshiped on Monday, Saturn was not worshiped on Saturday, and Apollo was not worshiped on any particular day. (His festivals were annual, not weekly.)

The seven-day week did not come into common use among the Romans until the third century, about the time the worship of the gods was disappearing. The change came as a result of the influence of Jews and Christians, not the other way around.

There was no special reverence for Sunday in the pagan world. The earliest Sunday legislation was enacted under Constantine I, A.D. 321. No legislation of earlier date on the division of the month is known. The pagans had to conform to the Christian day, not vice versa. The law was a matter of civil, not religious, obedience.

The planetary week, in which the days were named from their regents, Saturday, Sunday, and so forth, was an invention of the astrologers in the early second century B.C. They were astrological-astronomical, not religious.

The charge that "the pope changed the Sabbath" will not hold water. In the first place, the Sabbath was not changed; it was abandoned. In the second place, a careful study of Catholic dogma will reveal that the Roman Church claims to have instituted a new day of worship *in that the original apostles did so.* It does not make sense for Sabbatarians to quote papal authority on "Sabbath changing" when they believe almost nothing else claimed by the papacy.

To follow Armstrong is to follow the Law. It is to be debtor to do the whole Law. It is to fall from grace.

"Tell me, ye that desire to be under the law,

140

do ye not hear the law? For it is written, that Abraham had two sons, the one by a bondmaid, the other by a freewoman. But he who was of the bondwoman was born after the flesh; but he of the freewoman was by promise. Which things are an allegory: for these are the two covenants; the one from the mount Sinai, which gendereth to bondage, which is Agar. For this Agar is mount Sinai in Arabia, and answereth to Jerusalem which now is, and is in bondage with her children. But Jerusalem which is above is free, which is the mother of us all. For it is written, Rejoice, thou barren that bearest not; break forth and cry, thou that travailest not: for the desolate hath many more children than she which hath an husband. Now we, brethren, as Isaac was, are the children of promise. But as then he that was born after the flesh persecuted him that was born after the Spirit, even so it is now. Nevertheless what saith the scripture? Cast out the bondwoman and her son: for the son of the bondwoman shall not be heir with the son of the freewoman. So then, brethren, we are not children of the bondwoman, but of the free (Gal. 4:21-31).

6 PHONOLOGY OR "PHONY-OLOGY"?

Armstrongite etymology and phonology is not a study of language, the sounds of language, and the links between languages. It is a study in phoniness. The basic qualification of one who would follow Armstrongite phonology is an ignorance of languages in general and of the Hebrew language in particular.

There is no need to systematically examine each offering by Armstrong in this area. His teaching about "Saxons" and "Dan" will clearly expose the fabric of Armstrongite language studies.

> To Abraham, God said, "In ISAAC shall thy seed be called," and this name is repeated in Romans 9:7 and Hebrews 11:18. In Amos 7:16 they are called "The House of ISAAC."
> They were descended from Isaac, and therefore are Isaac's sons. Drop the "I" from "Isaac" (vowels are not used in Hebrew spelling), and we have the modern name, "SAAC'S SONS," or, as we spell it in shorter manner, "SAXONS!"[1]

This is standard British-Israelism.

Genesis 21:12 does not say that the seed of Abraham would be called "Isaac." It states that they would be called *in* Isaac; that is, through the genealogical line of Isaac. The text of Romans 9 is:

---

[1] *USBCP*, p. 116.

> Not as though the word of God hath taken
> none effect. For they are not all Israel, which are
> of Israel: Neither, because they are the seed of
> Abraham, are they all children: but in Isaac shall
> thy seed be called. *That is, They which are the
> children of the flesh, these are not the children
> of God:* but the children of the promise are
> counted for the seed (vv. 9:6-8).

Again, Armstrong depends upon his readers to take his word for what the Bible says and not to read it for themselves, even when he makes reference to a particular text. Armstrong cites the Genesis and Romans texts to prove that the name of fleshly Israel (i.e., Anglo-Saxons) is to be "Isaac." Paul cites the Genesis text and says it means that "they which are the children of the flesh, these are not the children of God." Precisely the *opposite* of what Armstrong is teaching from the same text. Romans 9 teaches that the true seed of Abraham, in or through Isaac, are the spiritual heirs, the church. According to Paul, Armstrongites are not the children of God, by their own argument; for they insist they are the children of the flesh.

Then follows the argument from etymology. He explains, "Vowels are not used in Hebrew spelling." Not true! It is true that vowels are not always *written* in Hebrew writing, but there never was a time when vowels were not used, in Hebrew or any other language. (Try to say "cat" without using a vowel.) The vowel points now used in Hebrew texts were inserted by numerous Hebrew scholars known as the Masoretes (fifth-fifteenth centuries A.D.). These annotations were made to indicate traditional pronunciation and intonation; that is, the vowel sounds traditionally used. The points did not create a system of vowels. They simply indicated a previous, largely unwritten, system of vowels.

Although there are certain links among all the members of the Western family of languages, there does not exist the kind of connection between English and Hebrew taught by Armstrong. English, a recent mongrelization of Saxon, Norman, Scandinavian, French, and later Spanish, has no more direct connection with Biblical Hebrew than has any other language.

But even if there had been a direct transition from Hebrew to English (which is absurd), it would not have permitted the kind of alterations that would make "Saxon" out of "Isaac's Sons." The convenient dropping of the "I" by Armstrong to get Saxon from Isaac's Sons is a piece of tomfoolery. There never was a time when vowels were not used in speaking. And all transition in language takes place in the speaking of the language, not the writing of it. Writing—that is, spelling, grammar, punctuation, and so forth—reflects the spoken form, and usually follows along at least a generation behind it.

And note that Armstrong does not drop all the vowels. He drops only the "I." The other vowel is allowed to stand. On what basis is the "I" dropped whereas the "a" survives? As a matter of fact, in the Hebrew spelling of Isaac the "a" sound is a vowel, but the letter transliterated into the English "I" is not a vowel at all. The transliteration of Isaac from the Hebrew is technically *yishaq*. Written vowelless it is *yshq*. The main part of the Hebrew sound that comes out "I" in Isaac is the letter *yod*, which, standing at the beginning of a word, is a *consonant.* Thus Armstrong "drops the vowels" on the basis of a transition in language, which is colossal ignorance, and as it comes out, the vowel point which *is* a vowel sound ("a") is allowed to stand, and the sound which is principally a consonant is dropped.

It is hard to believe that Armstrong is so ignorant of Hebrew. It is easier to believe that such constructions are designed to deceive.

The discovery of traces of Dan has been a favorite ploy of British-Israelism.

> In Genesis 49:17, Jacob, foretelling what should befall each of the tribes, says: "Dan shall be a serpent by the way." Another translation of

the original Hebrew is: "Dan shall be a serpent's trail."[2]

By citing "another translation" Armstrong leads the reader to see that the prophecy by Jacob did not mean that Dan would be a serpent coiling by the path in ambush. It means that Dan would be a serpent leaving a trail in the dust. British-Israelism has mapped that trail. Again Armstrong carefully avoids quoting the whole verse, which is:

> Dan shall be a serpent by the way, an adder in the path, that biteth the horse heels, so that his rider shall fall backward (Gen. 49:17).

The other "translation" notwithstanding, when one reads the prophecy in its entirety, the "serpent's trail" business goes up in smoke.

Everytime Armstrong finds the English *D* and the English *N* sounds within spitting distance of one another, he plants a flag there and pronounces it a waymark left by Dan (Lon*don*, *Den*mark, River *Don*, and so forth). To argue for Hebrew etymological connection on the basis of phonic similarity in English is to build a philological citadel on the foundation of a pun.

If E*din*burgh proves that Dan was in Scotland, then the *Dan*ikil tribe of North Africa are Danites as well. Other traces are Manasseh in *Man*churia, Ham in Birming*ham*, Asher in *Asia*, Simeon in *Siam*, and Korah in *Korea*. Armstrongite philology enjoys the intellectual stature of Mother Goose.

2 *USBCP*, p. 117.